THE STATE, CONCEPTUAL CHAOS, AND THE FUTURE OF INTERNATIONAL RELATIONS THEORY

New Books in the Series

- Exploring the Stability of Deterrence
  edited by Jacek Kugler and Frank C. Zagare

- Arms Transfers to the Third World: Probability Models of
  Superpower Decisionmaking *Gregory S. Sanjian*

- Nigeria and the International Capitalist System
  edited by Toyin Falola and Julius O. Ihonvbere

- Defining Political Development
  Stephen Chilton

- Science, Politics, and International Conferences:
  A Functional Analysis of the Moscow Political Science Congress
  Richard L. Merritt and Elizabeth C. Hanson

- The State, Conceptual Chaos, and the Future of
  International Relations Theory
  Yale H. Ferguson and Richard W. Mansbach

THE STATE, CONCEPTUAL CHAOS, AND THE FUTURE OF INTERNATIONAL RELATIONS THEORY

Yale H. Ferguson
Richard W. Mansbach

GSIS Monograph Series
in World Affairs

THE UNIVERSITY OF DENVER

Lynne Rienner Publishers • Boulder & London

The lines from W. H. Auden's poem "September 1, 1939" are reprinted with permission from *The English Auden: Poems, Essays, and Dramatic Writing 1927-1939*, edited by Edward Mendelson, © Random House, Inc.

Several short passages are reprinted with permission from *The Sociology of the State*, Bertrand Badie and Pierre Birnbaum (translated by Arthur Goldhammer), © The University of Chicago Press, 1983.

The authors are grateful to The University of South Carolina Press for permission to use material from *The Elusive Quest: Theory and International Politics*, Yale H. Ferguson and Richard W. Mansbach, © The University of South Carolina, 1988.

Published in the United States of America in 1989 by
Lynne Rienner Publishers, Inc.
1800 30th Street, Boulder, Colorado 80301

and in the United Kingdom by
Lynne Rienner Publishers, Inc.
3 Henrietta Street, Covent Garden, London WC2E 8LU

Library of Congress Cataloging-in-Publication Data

Ferguson, Yale H.
    The state, conceptual chaos, and the future of international
relations theory/by Yale H. Ferguson and Richard W. Mansbach.
      p.   cm.
    Bibliography: p.
    Includes index.
    ISBN 1-55587-144-5 (alk. paper)
    1. State, The—History. 2. International relations—History.
I. Mansbach, Richard W., 1943–   . II. Title.
JC325.F37 1989
320.1'09—dc19   88-29387
                                    CIP

British Cataloguing in Publication Data
A Cataloguing in Publication record for this book
is available from the British Library

Printed and bound in the United States of America

The paper used in this publication meets the requirements of
the American National Standard for Permanence of Paper for
Printed Library Materials Z39.48-1984

All I have is a voice
To unfold the folded lie,
The romantic lie in the brain
Of the sensual man-in-the-street
And the lie of Authority
Whose buildings grope the sky:
There is no such thing as the State. . . .

W.H. Auden, "September 1, 1939"

Contents

Introduction

In July 1985, we presented a paper entitled "The State as an Obstacle to International Theory" at the International Political Science Association World Congress in Paris; that paper eventually evolved into a chapter in a book, *The Elusive Quest: Theory and International Politics*,[1] and now into this considerably expanded version. A large audience received the orginal paper with—to say the least—general consternation. Until that experience we had not fully appreciated how attached, professionally and even passionately, so many scholars are to their own particular concepts of "the state."

By suggesting—as we shall again—that the concept has so many meanings that it is practically useless as an analytical tool and as a building-block for theory, we had managed to offend practically everyone. We agitated realists, neorealists, legalists, Marxists, neo-Marxists, quantifiers, traditional historicists, and, of course, practitioners who viewed themselves as surrogates of that which we were discussing. It was all great fun and seemed to offer eloquent testimony to the essential validity of our argument. For the most striking thing was that, although each commentator was entirely confident of his or her *own* notion of "the state," there was nothing remotely approaching a consensus in the hall. We concluded that David Held was correct in his observation: "There is nothing more central to political and social theory than the nature of the

1

state, and nothing more contested."[2]

Every discipline defines itself and is defined by others in terms of a shared set of assumptions and concepts. Those assumptions and concepts at once provide boundaries that distinguish that field of endeavor from others, and a research agenda for the future. Unfortunately, very few such shared assumptions and concepts have evolved in what is variously called "international," "interstate," "global," or "world" politics.

We are not suggesting that the road to international theory would be clear if only we could get around the concept of the state. The state is far from the only troublesome concept. However, the state is obviously a—if not *the*—key concept in the "emerging" discipline of international relations. And, insofar as it is not part of the solution to creating good theory, it is part of the problem—that is, an obstacle. In practice, the state concept virtually defines the boundaries of whatever discipline of international relations exists. Without the concept to fall back on, scholars would have to abandon the claim that there is something unique about the "international" or "interstate" realm.

On the other hand, the *root* problem in building international theory is not merely fuzzy concepts, but something much more fundamental: the root problem is the way that theory in international politics evolves generally. This process is discussed at length in *The Elusive Quest*.

ONE

The State as a
Normative Concept

The state concept is so central to international relations that there is no possibility of developing unified and cumulative international theory in the absence of general agreement as to what the concept connotes.[3] If the state is a variable and not a constant, very little of our past experience in international relations is likely to be relevant to understanding the present or future. Since historically the concept has held widely different connotations for scholars, it is likely that conclusions drawn in each era about political behavior are unique.

But more important to consider is one of the *reasons* consensual meaning has eluded thinkers and practitioners. The concept of the state—like virtually all concepts in the field of international relations and many in the social sciences generally—is drenched with normative connotations. As such, the state concept can be observed historically, to clarify how our views of the world have evolved and to afford insights into various processes of cooperation and conflict; but it will frustrate those who dare believe we can use it as our cousins in the natural sciences use concepts. In its many manifestations, concepts like the state tend to reflect the different "truths" of different true believers rather than the simple truth that the empiricist assumes awaits him.

Efforts to define the state have inevitably combined views of what it is with what it ought to be, views conditioned by

3

context-bound issues of practical political significance. Competing theories of the state, in effect, invariably come perilously near to being competing ideologies. For Aristotle, for example, the notion of the state was inseparable from that of the Greek *polis*. F.H. Hinsley comments:

> Writing in the fourth century B.C., at the end of a long development that had culminated in the previous century in the civilization of the classical city-state, [Aristotle] was able to feel that "man is by nature a *polis*-being" and to conclude that the political society of the *polis* was the highest form of human association and commmunity. He made no distinction, however, between the community and the state; his word *polis* which we translate as state did not distinguish between the two.[4]

For Romans, the state evolved from the *polis* of the core city of Rome itself into a vast empire with an emperor, who in later stages was seen by many as being both "above the law" and divine. When the Roman Empire gave way to the "barbarians," as J.M. Wallace-Hadrill observes, kingship "lost some of its ancient prestige" and persons "tended increasingly to organize their lives on a local basis" under local magnates or lords.[5]

For Thomas Aquinas and his contemporaries in the Middle Ages, there were, depending upon one's perspective, many overlapping states or none—a diffuse and fragmented hierarchy of authority, with God at the pinnacle, through pope and emperor and local monarchs, down to the single town, manor, or cloister. However, there also gradually developed what Susan Reynolds views as various horizontal bonds of collective association.[6] Wallace-Hadrill notes that out of the barbarian invasions, notwithstanding all the institutional diffuseness and the fact that they did not necessarily expect to be ruled by native dynasties, "the states of medieval Europe had emerged." "There was no longer any doubt," he says, "that, despite Empire and Papacy, France, Germany, Italy, Spain, Scandinavia and England were going their own ways, speaking their own languages and interpreting the past in different senses."[7] Of course, there still often remained a question as to which of "their own languages" was to be *the* national language, not to mention the transnational language of the church or of diplomacy conducted by aristocrats.

Whatever their precise condition, they were communities of

sorts, larger than Aristotle's *polis*, yet far more circumscribed than the Roman Church or Empire. Reynolds writes:

> The community of the realm was . . . not . . . a peculiarly English concept, . . . It was something much older and more general. Any kingdom which survived did so because it was in some sense felt to be a community. That is not to say that enduring kingdoms were in reality the political manifestation of peoples of common descent and inherited common culture—what people today usually call nations. People thought of them as that, for law was the basis of politics and the metaphor of kingship was strong and emotive. All the same, kingdoms were created and preserved not by kinship but by government, and government of an essentially public character. The loyalty people felt to their government was on a different level from that to their family, their lord, or their locality. . . . [T]here was no idea that sovereignty should be single and precisely located: government consisted of layers of authority, and loyalties were attracted to each layer accordingly.[8]

Moreover, by the beginning of the fourteenth century, in most of western Europe "people . . . believed that government depended on consultation and consent, and that its object was to achieve a harmonious consensus in accordance with the custom and law of the whole community."[9] On the other hand, harmonious consensus was exceedingly difficult to achieve when the many "layers" of medieval society were regularly engaged in political and even violent conflict: pope vs. emperor, king vs. pope and/or emperor, king vs. leading nobles,[10] nobles vs. nobles, towns and/or peasants vs. local lords. Was this community, anarchy, or something else fundamentally unique? Was there an "interstate" system or not?

The fifteenth and sixteenth centuries, by contrast, witnessed the rise throughout much of Europe of putatively "absolute" monarchies, along with standing armies, a permanent bureaucracy, national taxation, a codified law, more clearly delineated territorial frontiers, and the beginnings of a unified market.[11] As Roger King astutely points out, "it was crisis and instability in international affairs that, alongside dynastic ambition, encouraged the territorial consolidation and centralizing pressures." The "great restorers of internal order . . . were given a strong impetus by the various crises of the late fourteenth century—war, disease, economic stagnation—which considerably weakened the lords of the manor."[12]

The new monarchies, which enjoyed access to the resources of large territories, were unprecedented military machines, a development fully appreciated by Machiavelli following the French invasion of Italy in 1492. Michael Mann has concluded that some 75 to 90 percent of state finances between 1130 to 1815 went to the acquisition and use of military force; and he observes that, although such force obviously played a role in "domestic repression," the "chronology of its development" was "almost entirely determined by the incidence of international war."[13] Perry Anderson characterizes the absolutist states as "machines built for the battlefield," and he regards it as "significant that the first regular national tax to be imposed in France, the *taille royale*, was levied to finance the first regular military units in Europe."[14] In Bill Jordan's view, the absolutist "state arose from new productive relations, and—even if it played a very limited role in actually organizing production or exchange—was primarily a means of protecting these relations in a given territory, both from the depredations of internal deviants, and from those of external enemies."[15] In a word, economic and military power evolved in unison.

Some of the consequences of these developments were that a more clearly demarcated and somewhat more homogenous set of political units emerged on the map of Europe, a formal diplomatic system developed, and trade expanded under the doctrine of mercantilism.[16] In addition, as King observes:

> [T]he influence of Italian humanism and the more complicated effects of the Reformation strengthened the power of the secular authority against that of the Church. The religious unity of the Christian community was fragmented, the theocratic basis of the Holy Roman Empire was undermined, and the idea of the charitable role of the secular authorities was established. Religious upheaval in the sixteenth and seventeenth centuries sustained princely power.[17]

Dramatic shifts in prevailing theories of authority —its sources and its nature—accompanied and, of course, to some extent accelerated all of these developments, many of which involved the search for and struggle over the roots of legitimacy for leadership.

After the decline of Rome, in the words of Reinhard Bendix, the "Western church put the king under God's law as interpreted by the church; the Eastern church accepted the emperor as representing Christ on earth." The notion that the king was "God's Anointed" on earth "replaced the earlier belief in the divine origin of the charismatic lineage." Yet it is significant that Charlemagne, as early as the eighth century, insisted on adding to his title "by the Grace of God" (*Dei gratia*), "thus appearing to give the monarch a position based on divine inspiration."[18] Conflict between religious and secular authorities was virtually inevitable from the outset (even though dual authority was often vested in the same individual) and came to the fore in the Middle Ages over such issues as the appointment of key clergy. The dual papacy, widespread corruption and impiety at all levels of the Roman church, Henry VIII's establishment of the Church of England, and the broader Reformation—all helped pave the way for general acceptance of the revised doctrine that kings had a "divine right" to rule that came directly from God and was entirely independent of recognition by the church.

Ironically, however, in western Europe even as kings gradually gained their independence from the church, they were confronted by new challenges arising from the changing nature of the societies over which they ruled. The weakening of the traditional landed aristocracy, symbolized by the end of serfdom, was to some degree offset by the rise of an entrepreneurial "middle class" in town and country. The revival of Roman law began in Italy in the twelfth century and spread across Europe by the end of the Middle Ages. This phenomenon—what Perry Anderson rightly terms "one of the great cultural movements of the age"—in its civil law dimension "was fundamentally propitious to the growth of free capital in town and country" because it gave unequivocal support to the concept of private property.[19] On the other hand, and not without a measure of internal contradiction, the remnants of Roman public law vastly enhanced the role of kings. Of this, Anderson writes:

> [T]he enhancement of private property from below was matched by the increase of public authority from above, embodied in the discretionary power of the royal ruler. The Absolutist States in the West based their novel aims on classical precedents: Roman law was the most powerful intellectual weapon available for their typical programme of territorial integration and administrative centralism. It was no accident, in fact, that the one mediaeval monarchy which

had achieved complete emancipation from any representative
or corporate restraints was the Papacy, which had been the
first political system of feudal Europe to utilize Roman
jurisprudence wholesale, with the codification of canon law in
the 12th and 13th centuries.[20]

The great political theorists of the Renaissance and the
ancien régime reacted in their writings to the conflicts they
knew firsthand. Niccolo Machiavelli's idea of the state and its
prince drew its inspiration from the Italian city-state universe
in which he lived and from a sense of Italian patriotism and,
more immediately, from his urgent desire to secure a position at
the Medici court in Florence. He was the first theorist in
modern times to suggest that the ruler was essentially above
the law and that the power of the state which the ruler
embodied "was something which, if not an end in itself, at least
obeyed its own rules and had its own *raison d'être*."[21]
Nevertheless, the French occupation of Italy subsequently
convinced Machiavelli (*Discourses*) of the need for republican-
limited government, which form he believed was the only one
capable of building sufficient community solidarity to resist
external threats.

Practice also shaped the ideas of Jean Bodin, who is usually
credited with having articulated the first full-blown notion of
state "sovereignty." F.H. Hinsley observes that "Bodin's book
was a direct outcome of the confusion brought about by civil and
religious wars in a France which had known no peace between
the conflicts arising from the dissolution of its feudalized
segmentary structure and the onset of the Reformation in the
form of a new kind of rebellion against the state."[22] Likewise,
Thomas Hobbe's *Leviathan* was the product of his preoccupation
with civil strife in England, which must indeed have seemed a
"Warre of every one against every one." The only answer, he
insisted, was the creation of the state as an "Artificiall Man,"
"One Person" ruling over a "Multitude of men" with absolute,
sovereign power.

One cannot begin to understand the state theories of
Machiavelli, Bodin, or Hobbes without appreciating the context
in which they wrote and the values which they held. And it is
only as context and values changed that the version of the state
embraced by John Locke and many of his contemporaries could
emerge.

In practice, absolute monarchs found themselves facing not

only traditional challenges from the nobility, but also increasing demands from "below" in a society that was growing ever more complex. A colleague in English literature tells us that the first time the term "the state" came into general use in England was during the Cromwell era when the crown's properties were seized and the Cromwellians scratched their round heads trying to decide to whom or to what the properties now belonged. In the same vein, James Anderson observes that "the 'Great Rebellion' of the 1640s did reverse the advance of absolutism and it shifted the balance away from the monarchy and aristocracy in favour of the commercialized gentry and merchants, and the realm of 'civil society' in general."[23] Writing about the time of the Glorious Revolution of 1688, which imposed new constitutional limits on the English crown, Locke advanced the view that only the People were sovereign, with full powers under natural law. These powers, in turn, were partially delegated by contract to government for certain benefits, and the contract was revocable if and when government failed to fulfill its end of the bargain satisfactorily.

Nearly a century later (1776) Adam Smith also defended the notion of a liberal state in which the People reigned and were allowed to go about their business under *laissez-faire* economic policies. The perspective of Locke and Smith coincided with the political and economic interests of a rising "middle class"—and also captured the imagination of upper-crust revolutionaries and capitalists in the United States. (Contract became the watchword in more ways than one.) It also reflected an era of relative personal security and prosperity and growing optimism about the future.

Others in Great Britain debated the purposes that a limited state should serve. Jeremy Bentham and James Mill based their "utilitarian" position—that government should secure the "greatest good for the greatest number"—on the behavioral thesis that humans act to satisfy desire and to avoid pain. Nonetheless, as Held points out, Bentham and Mill, reflecting the prejudices of the early nineteenth century, were only "reluctant democrats" and saw no inconsistency in excluding from the franchise all laborers and women. James Mill's son, John Stuart Mill, was, however, a much less ambiguous advocate of full democracy and saw the mission of representative government as the "highest and harmonious" development of individual capabilities.[24]

The *ancien régime* lasted longer on the continent than in England, and the legacy of the French Revolution was as much authoritarian as it was democratic. Rousseau's vague concepts of absolute popular sovereignty and a state which was the embodiment of a platonic "general will" formed part of the background of the Revolution and had enduring influence. "This view," in Jordan's words, "contributed to the Jacobin notion of a centralised state, advocated by Marat and Robespierre, which formed the basis of the French constitution of 1793. It influenced the centralism of Napoleon's constitution and administration, which in turn shaped the French state throughout the nineteenth century."25   Napoleon himself, as E.H. Carr argues, gave a major thrust to the identification of the state with the nation:

> Napoleon, by posing as the champion and mandatory of the emancipated French nation, made himself the chief missionary of modern nationalism. He was in many senses the first 'popular' dictator. Intellectually, the transition from Frederick [the Great] to Napoleon was paralleled by the transition from Gibbon to Burke, or from Goethe and Lessing to Herder and Schiller; the cosmopolitanism of the Enlightenment was replaced by the nationalism of the Romantic movement.26

The impact of the Romantic era is evident on Hegel's view of the state as a moral idea, the highest realization of self. Hegel's conception later meshed nicely with Social Darwinism and found a particularly nasty echo in German extremist glorifiers of the state like Treitschke—and finally, of course, Hitler.

Karl Marx's writings on the state reflected both the rise to power of Louis Napoleon Bonaparte and the urban proletariat that Marx saw, growing and restive, all around him in the industrializing Europe of his day. Held correctly emphasizes that "Marx left an ambiguous heritage, never fully reconciling his understanding of the state as an instrument of class domination with his acknowledgement that the state might also have significant political independence." All that was entirely clear was that for Marx, in contrast to Hegel, there was nothing inherently "moral" about the state. In *The Eighteenth Brumaire of Louis Bonaparte,* Marx portrayed the state as an immense and powerful bureaucracy that has relative autonomy from bourgeois society, even though its policies cannot fail to be compatible over the longer run with the interests of manufacturers and traders.[27] In the *Communist Manifesto* and other works, however, Marx sharpened his contention that the state is the instrument of a dominant economic class and added yet another confusion—one that would continue to bedevil socialists and communists of all stripes—that the state in the hands of the working class would eventually "wither away."

Outside of Europe, as well, the state concept has been the subject of ideological disputes responsive to prevailing circumstances. Confucian thought, for example, held that China—and, indeed, all the earth—was united under an emperor who was the Son of Heaven. We have very little of Confucius's original writings and must depend on subsequent codifications, which perhaps lend support to the view advanced by John A. Hall (drawing on Max Weber) that the state itself was responsible for creating the bulk of Confucian doctrine. Be that as it may, the principal alternative to Confucianism as a political philosophy was Legalism, a doctrine maintaining that force alone held the state together. According to Hall:

> Interestingly, . . . the doctrine was not perhaps the one most perfectly suited to imperial rule. Legalism had been preferred by the first Ch'in emperor, but his brutalities, especially the burning of Confucian scholars together with their books, ruled this doctrine out of court thereafter. As it is, Confucianism supported the state but did so only as long as it was successful: the withdrawal of the mandate of heaven could be proclaimed, as most emperors realised.[28]

Nevertheless, the ideal of Chinese unity persisted, even, as was so often the case, when China was politically fragmented.

The early Indian conception of the state, probably articulated for the first Mauryan emperor circa 300 B.C. by his adviser, Chanakya Kautilya, saw the emperor as essentially an executive for Brahmin law and envisaged realist-style power relations prevailing among local rulers. The *Arthashastra*, an extraordinary piece of analysis attributed to Kautilya, is often compared with justification to Machiavelli's *The Prince*. Adda B. Bozeman comments: "In its brash and unscrupulous espousal of success as the true measure of statesmanship, the work is a reflection of India's long history of practically continuous war, strife, and division."[29] Some years later, when the Emperor Asoka (272–231 B.C.) was converted to Buddhism,

Kautilya's ideas gave way to the notion of a peaceful empire under an emperor who was the defender and chief missionary of a universalist faith.

This blurring of the lines between state and religion, as in contemporary Iran, has been a prominent feature of the Islamic world from the appearance of the prophet Mohammed to the present day. There has been an almost continual tension between the secular state in its local manifestations and the state seen by the faithful as a servant of Islam.

Contemporary analyses of the state have been no less infused by normative commitment than these historical examples. Woodrow Wilson, for example, was firmly convinced that the disaster of World War I had accelerated a worldwide trend toward political democracy, national self-determination, and international cooperation. Another world war later, realists like E.H. Carr, Hans Morgenthau, Reinhold Neibuhr, and Kenneth W. Thompson inveighed strongly against such "idealism."

In Morgenthau's view,[30] for example, human nature is essentially imperfect and intensely selfish; and the international system, partly as a consequence, is basically anarchic, highly competitive, and amoral. In an environment like this, argues Morgenthau, each state has no choice but to pursue its "national interest" defined in terms of "power." Acting for the state are "rational" decisionmakers who, if they follow Morgenthau's prescription, will readily recognize that other states, as well as their own, have interests and thus introduce an element of restraint into an otherwise dog-eat-dog world. Morgenthau's ideal (he would not pardon that characterization), rather like Henry Kissinger's, is a diplomacy devoid of ideological crusades—tough and determined, yet moderate, pragmatic, and prudent.

Of course, as many analysts have pointed out, Morgenthau's basic concepts like "national interest" and "power" are inherently subjective, and this seriously undermines the explanatory power of realism as "objective" theory. Realism's extraordinary appeal, especially among the immediate post-World War II generation of U.S. policymakers, may owe partly to the fact that there was (and is) something ego-gratifying, macho, and even romantic about picturing oneself as advancing the national interest in a struggle for power. In addition, his ringing endorsement of a characteristically, albeit not exclusively, U.S. penchant for pragmatism allows policymakers to hide from themselves any troubling questions about the values that are being advanced by their policies. Morgenthau himself admits:

> Political realism contains not only a theoretical but also a normative element. It knows that political reality is replete with contingencies and systematic irregularities and points to the typical influences they exert upon foreign policy. . . . Political realism wants the photographic picture of the political world to resemble as much as possible its painted portrait. Aware of the inevitable gap between good—that is, rational—foreign policy and foreign policy as it actually is, political realism maintains not only that theory must focus upon the rational elements of political reality, but also that foreign policy ought to be rational in view of its own moral and practical purposes. Hence, it is no argument against the theory presented . . . that actual foreign policy does not or cannot live up to it.[31]

In fairness, however, the degree of subjectivity in Morgenthau's concepts is no greater than that found elsewhere in the literature.

For a time, however, except for die-hard realists, the concept of the state fell out of intellectual fashion—only to return in recent years with what is surely not its last hurrah. In 1968, J. P. Nettl observed: "The concept of the state is not much in vogue in the social sciences right now. Yet it retains a skeletal, ghostly existence largely because, for all the changes in emphasis and interest in research, the thing exists and no amount of conceptual restructuring can dissolve it."[32] Stephen D. Krasner saw much the same trend: "From the late 1950s until the mid-1970s, the term state virtually disappeared from the professional academic lexicon. Political scientists wrote about governments, political development, interest groups, voting, legislative behavior, leadership, and bureaucratic politics, almost everything but 'the state'."[33]

Why this downgrading of the state? For one thing, there was increasing recognition that the realists' world of objective national interests and putatively non-ideological behavior is as much a normative conception as Wilson's League of Nations. Analysts began asking realists hard questions like "whose national interest?" and "power for what?" and "isn't ideology part of power?" An acceptance of reductionism began to overcome theorists' natural preference for parsimony.

As Krasner's description of research concerns suggests, many scholars started to peer within the "black box" or "billiard ball" of the state, explicitly or implicitly questioning its autonomy and stressing the degree to which policy outcomes are shaped by domestic political actors and processes. Consequently, boundaries between intra- and interstate politics grew murky, and differences between government and state assumed more than legal importance. Alternatively, some of the same scholars and others emphasized the constraints on state autonomy emanating from the international environment—from the basic structure of the international system, international law, a great variety of international governmental and nongovernmental actors (IGOs and INGOs), economic interdependence, and "regimes." In the sense that the second perspective entailed an "international" emphasis, it was reminiscent of the Wilsonian idealism against which the realists had harangued. However, that is where the similarity ended.

The proponents of what might be called the new internationalism were a disparate group, including Marxist, neo-Marxist, and/or *dependencia* theorists, as well as theorists who were responsive to the fact that the apparently reduced salience of Cold War issues in the late 1960s and early 1970s produced greater attention to and interest in other pressing global issues. Such "post-realist" scholars were especially preoccupied with issues of international political economy such as resource allocation, recession, monetary instability, trade, transnational corporations, and environmental decay. Temporarily, at least, the state as traditionally conceived was no longer the principal focus of analysis, and the familiar issue of "power and peace" was no longer seen as necessarily delimiting the boundaries of international relations scholarship. Looking back at the previous decade, Krasner aptly declared in 1976: "In recent years, students of international relations have multinationalized, transnationalized, bureaucratized, and transgovernmentalized the state until it has virtually ceased to exist as an analytic construct."[34] Like other realists, he rued this trend and sought to counterattack.

If this was the situation in the mid-1970s, Krasner and others subsequently succeeded in resurrecting the notion of state autonomy. In their view, the state has significant resources of its own that often allow it to overcome constraints arising from both the domestic and international environments. Krasner's 1984 assessment was that "the agenda is already changing." Reviewing several important works relevant to this subject, he predicted: "'The state' will once again become a major concern of scholarly discourse."[35] So it has. One current fashion, "neorealism," involves, among other things, an effort to find a middle ground between obsession with the state and ignoring it completely. The so-called "crisis of the state" has moved beyond discussion mainly among political economists to become a principal concern of other scholars as well.

The renewed attention paid to the concept of the state has by no means lifted the fog of ambiguity surrounding it. Is the ill-defined entity autonomous? Unfortunately, there is not even full agreement on the meaning of "autonomy." Furthermore, while the phenomena of state (however defined) and autonomy (however defined) may have been underrated in the haste to give adequate weight to domestic and systemic constraints, important constraints do continue to derive from other actors/levels. The state's surrogates may well be the primary actors in international affairs, but they are not the only significant units of analysis. Recognizing the essential validity of this familiar statement, however, is far from being able to generalize with precision about the relationships involved. Although neorealists are attempting a synthesis, we have little reason to expect that a satisfactory one will be achieved. Kenneth Waltz, Robert Keohane, and others acknowledge a debt to realism but are otherwise light-years apart in their main concerns and approaches. Indeed, conceptual consensus would probably impose insufferable constraints upon their scholarship, requiring theoretical compromises that would test everyone's good will.

TWO

The Historical State

Since the absence of a consensus regarding the state concept inhibits the development of international relations theory, it might seem that an analysis of the historical roots of the phenomenon could help us identify the essential qualities of a state. But in fact, such an analysis offers little solace to the investigator, who will discover that, while there have existed since prehistoric times self-conscious subgroupings able to distinguish themselves from other groupings and conduct relations with them, there is no agreement that such entities have always been states. On the other hand, those who view the state as the relatively recent outcome of a period of Western political development run the risk not only of underestimating or ignoring earlier entities, but also of assuming the nonexistence of international relations until "modern" times. "If this is the actual history of the state," declares Sabino Cassese acerbically, "there is no need to disturb Plato and Aristotle in a search for the origin of the concept of the state unless we want to attribute to them, and to other thinkers who followed them, extraordinary abilities to foresee the future."[36]

By contrast, if the observer concludes that the state is an historically omnipresent phenomenon, he is confronted with a bewildering array of entities with so little in common that it becomes necessary to adopt highly abstract and effectively nonoperational definitions of the phenomenon. As abstraction

17

increases, the entity as a unit of analysis and corporate actor tends to vanish. In J.W. Burton's conception the state tends to dissolve into "linked systems and their administrative controls"[37] or some so-called "structural-functional" entity with no clear objective referent.

In reality, the difficulty in identifying the origins of the state may pose less of an historical than a conceptual problem. In other words, whether one conceives the state as having always existed or having been born in a particular era depends largely on one's definition of the state. Donald J. Puchala suggests "the first questions we must ask about the modern state are: What is it? and What are its origins? These questions answer each other."[38] Unfortunately, that is exactly what they do *not* do, since questions are not answers, and neither question *has* a satisfactory answer (as we shall attempt to explain).

Puchala's questions do, however, help to reveal the circularity of the problem we face. One cannot point to the historical origins of the state entity unless one can identify and operationalize the phenomenon that is being sought, and history does not afford an example that one would feel confident of offering as a "state for all seasons." This problem is discernible in the argument of two eminent French scholars, Bertrand Badie and Pierre Birnbaum:

> [T]he writer who wishes to treat the concept of the state faces a dilemma: either he must settle for a broad and therefore useless definition of the state or he must concede that "the state" is not a universal concept but rather the product of a specific historical crisis to which different premodern societies are vulnerable in different degrees. . . . On the other hand, we do not wish to argue that the state is peculiar to a single country or even to a small number of countries. Our point is simply this: in each society, particular historical processes foster state building to a greater or lesser degree. . . .
>
> The sociology of the state should . . . be careful to avoid . . . the conclusion that once the state is established, its nature and form are determined and will never change. In particular, we think it would be useful to study the conditions under which one type of state is transformed into another.[39]

However, if the state is not a "universal concept" but "the product of a specific historical crisis," how are we to assess the "greater or lesser degree" of "state building" in each society, much less, meaningfully, to typologize "states" and study the dynamics of their transformation?

Anthropologist Ronald Cohen runs into similar difficulties in the course of maintaining that "the state" had its origins in both social conflict (competition over scarce resources) and integration (benefits flowing from centralized authority):

> It is now becoming clear that there are multiple roads to statehood, that whatever sets off the process tends as well to set off other changes which, no matter how different they are to begin with, all tend to produce similar results. It is this similarity of result, I believe, that has clouded the issue of causality. Similar results—the state—imply common antecedents. Unfortunately, as the data are compared, as more cases appear in the literature, historical sequences support the notion of multiple and varied causes producing similar effects.[40]

Cohen's principal focus is on the "early state." He says: "Early states as far removed as Incan Peru, ancient China, Egypt, early Europe, and precolonial West Africa exhibit striking similarities. Thus the state as a form of organization is an emergent selective force that has sent humankind along a converging path."[41] Cohen acknowledges that "[h]omo sapiens has evolved a number of quite different and distinct political systems; one of these is the state." Moreover, "[f]rom this baseline of agreement, our notions about what to emphasize in a definition of 'state' begin to diverge sharply." He himself lists three classes of definitions.[42] How, then, can we be confident that the "similar results" of "multiple and varied causes" which he has identified are, in fact, "the state"? We certainly do not share that confidence.

Jonathan Haas's analysis of the "prehistoric state" is worth reviewing at length because it illustrates so well just how uncoordinated efforts have been to achieve understanding of the phenomenon's origins.

> [T]he first problem that needs to be confronted concerns the concept of the "state" itself. The myriad definitions presented in the literature tend to be either idiosyncratic or tied to a particular theoretical perspective....
>
> First, "state" is seen as representing the discrete complex of social institutions that operate together to govern a particular, highly evolved society. Under this conceptual-

ization, *the* state operates as a concrete entity within the social whole. Lenin, for example, argues that "the state is an organ of class *domination,*" . . .

The second notion of "state" sees it as referring to a particular *kind* of society characterized by specific attributes. In an evolutionary sense, this conception uses "state" as a label to classify societies that have reached a particular level of cultural development. . . .

Finally, "state" is used in a way that is somewhat complementary to the second usage. Specifically, it is used to simply identify individual bounded societies that are characterized by a "state" level of organization. In this sense, a "state" is analogous to a "tribe" or a "chiefdom." For example, one might refer to the Aztec *state* or the Zulu *state*, just as one might refer to the Zuni *tribe* or the Kwakuitl *chiefdom*. In contrast to the idea of the state being a part of a society, the third conception sees the state as the entire society.

These three notions of "state" do refer to different things, and lack of awareness of the distinctions between them has introduced a degree of confusion in the literature. What is one person's "state" is another person's "government" and vice versa. (Emphasis added)[43]

The implication appears to be that a state can be *any* form of political organization, and we are left in the dark about the level of organization necessary for an entity to qualify for statehood.

Haas's own definition is closer to the second in his list, yet he is unable to dismiss competing conceptualizations. He insists that the state represents a clear stage in political evolution, characterized by a rapid centralization, especially of economic power, and of ideological and physical power as well; and by the development of new territorial boundaries and more formal institutions of government. Nonetheless, in a recent, edited volume, he acknowledges that even his own contributors are not all using the same definitions of "state," and he reflects on the implications of this situation:

[A]re the researchers [looking at different cases] really talking about the same thing? Probably not. Is one definition and the accompanying analysis "right" and the other "wrong"? Probably not. The polities themselves remain the same, regardless of the terms that are applied to them, and the validity of the scientific inquiry into the nature of those polities need not be affected by the definition of analytical terms. ("A rose by any other name smells as sweet.")

However, conflicting definitions can lead to confusing and unproductive debates over the "origins" of the *first* state in a particular world area. As with the concept of "culture," it is probably not possible to generate a meaningful definition of the concept "state" which will be universally accepted by all archaeologists, anthropologists, political scientists, and so on. . . . [W]e must recognize that there are alternative working definitions.[44]

Haas concludes that one must get past the state concept by means of a working definition in order to get on with productive analysis. The present authors would certainly agree that a working definition is all that can be achieved, although we are less sanguine about the analytical consequences. The nature of polities may be the same in the mind of some supposedly objective observer regardless of the concepts applied. However, since no objective observer can be found, our perceptions of polities are mightily effected by the subjective concepts we use, and lack of consensus as to concepts drastically limits comparative analysis. If the polities are the same regardless, one might argue, why not just label them "polities," abandon the hopelessly controversial state concept, and move on? Again, is not "the state" actually an obstacle to theory? (Incidentally, with apologies to Haas and Shakespeare, gardeners will affirm that some hybrid roses do not, in fact, smell all that "sweet." What, then, makes them "roses"—different from lilacs that do?)

Let us examine how the authors of two other works treat the state as an historical and even pre-historical phenomenon, while failing to denote that which they are seeking to describe. In the view of Ernest Gellner:

Mankind has passed through three fundamental stages in its history: the pre-agrarian, the agrarian, and the industrial. Hunting and gathering bands were and are too small to allow the kind of political division of labour which constitutes the state; and so, for them, the question of the state, of a stable specialized order-enforcing institution, does not really arise. By contrast, most, but by no means all, agrarian societies have been state-endowed. . . . They differ a great deal in their form. The agrarian phase of human history is the period during which, so to speak, the very existence of the state is an option. . . . During the hunting-gathering stage, the option was not available.

By contrast, in the post-agrarian, industrial age there is,

again, no option; but now the *presence*, not the absence of the
state is inescapable. Paraphrasing Hegel, once none had the
state, then some had it, and finally all have it. The form it
takes still remains variable. There are some traditions of
social thought—anarchism, Marxism—which hold that even,
or especially, in an industrial order the state is dispensable, at
least under favourable conditions or under conditions due to
be realized in the fullness of time. There are obvious and
powerful reasons for doubting this.[45]

Gellner purports to see the appearance of "the state" at a
relatively early, "agrarian" stage of human history. This is not,
however, a genuine empirical claim. Since Gellner admits the
form of the "state" to be "variable" at any stage, the only
apparent requirement is that the entity involved must have
been a "stable specialized order-enforcing institution." Yet that
is a characteristic of polities *sui generis*!

For their part, Badie and Birnbaum assert:

> To be sure, centralized political systems have been a feature
> not only of modern but also of many ancient or classical
> societies. The novelty of modern times is that exceptions to
> the law of centralization are no longer tolerated, the division of
> labor in modern society being such that none can escape the
> need for coordination through a centralized political structure
> or structures. But this is the only common feature of modern
> political systems, and as soon as the political sociologist begins
> to concern himself with history or simply with the empirical
> data he is forced to admit that political centralization may
> take many forms and that the particular form that emerges in
> any given case is largely related to cultural and conjunctural
> factors: state-building is only one form of political
> centralization among others, and the models followed in
> building states vary widely from one society to the next.[46]

According to Badie and Birnbaum, the state is not omnipresent
and is clearly demarcated from and predates society:

> Even in the West, however, civil society has at times been able
> to make do without a state. It has often been able to organize
> itself and by doing so to prevent the development of a state
> with some claim to the right to wield absolute power.
> Wherever a state exists, the entire social system is affected.
> Civil society invariably organizes around the state once a state
> has come into existence. . . . Class relations vary widely

depending on whether there is a highly institutionalized state or a mere political center whose main function is to coordinate the activities of civil society.[47]

What, then, do Badie and Birnbaum regard as a true "state" as distinct from a "mere political center"? The closest they come to such a definition is the following:

> [T]he true state (as distinguished from what is merely the center of a centralized political system) is one that has achieved a certain level of differentiation, autonomy, universality, and institutionalization. These features remain characteristic, even if . . . all of the features named may coexist with dedifferentiation and epigenesis.[48]

So a "true state" has "certain characteristic features"—or does it? If only selected entities are "true states," what does that imply for other entities that behave in state-like ways? In the end, Badie and Birnbaum settle on France as "the ideal type of the state" or "the state model," arguing that the political center of that country carried out the "process of differentiation and institutionalization"[49] further than others in Europe because it needed to do so to overcome greater resistance from feudal vestiges in French society. [50] And they apply the same categories to analyzing contemporary Europe:

> It is still possible even today to distinguish between political systems in which there is both a center and a state (France), a state but no center (Italy), a center but no true state (Great Britain and the United States), and neither a center nor a true state (Switzerland). In the first two cases the state dominates civil society and is responsible for its organization albeit in different degrees. In the last two cases civil society organizes itself. It is therefore possible to distinguish between societies in which the state attempts to run the social system through a powerful bureaucracy (of which France is the ideal type, with Prussia, Spain, and Italy exhibiting similar trajectories) and societies in which there is no need for a strong state and governing bureaucracy because civil society is capable of organizing itself (of which Great Britain is the ideal type, with the United States and "consociational democracies" . . . such as Switzerland exhibiting similar trajectories).[51]

Badie and Birnbaum place less emphasis on the state's

autonomy from societal influences than on society's lack of autonomy from organizational influences emanating from the political system's "center" (where one exists).

Even if Badie and Birnbaum's "true state" has not always existed, divisions between rulers and ruled and a consciousness of various forms of "we-they" distinctions definitely have. Although it is apparently true, as Morton H. Fried observes, that "the ancients left no self-conscious history of the evolution of their earliest states,"[52] there have clearly been territorial-political entities—some of substantial size and/or authority—in the global system for many thousands of years. As Oran Young observes: "Over the bulk of recorded history, man has organized himself for political purposes on bases other than those now subsumed under the concepts 'state' and 'nation-state'."[53] Whether one chooses to term them "chiefdoms," "empires," "city-states," "principalities," "states," or something else seems to us to rest exclusively on the nature of the entity in question and on one's choice of definitions.

This last statement is a truism, but it highlights, first, the important fact that early entities evinced several or many of the characteristics customarily associated with the "modern state": territory, executives, legislatures, judges, a bureaucracy, taxes, armies, interest groups, social classes; as well as problems of succession, peer-polity and center-periphery relations, alliances, wars, trade, ecology. The list could go on.[54] In other words, there are functional similarities (perhaps even homologies) among such units. At a minimum, there appears to be some functional continuity over time among the institutional arrangements made by human beings to govern themselves and act as their surrogates.

Second, institutional artifacts from every stage of human political evolution may still be found in the present "industrial" or "post-industrial" era, even as the "progress" of industrial-ization has varied tremendously from place to place. Just as there are a few remaining pockets of Stone Age culture and many predominately agrarian societies, so, too, do there continue to be tribes, city-states, surprisingly autonomous cities, and other political subdivisions (like "states" in the U.S. federal system), monarchs (albeit mostly enfeebled), popes and patriarchs, myriad ethnicities, latent and more substantial "nations," complex bureaucracies, classes and masses, a host of interest groups, political parties, transnational corporations, transgovernmental organizations, alliances, ideological empires, and other putative neo-imperialisms. To borrow a felicitous phrase that Charles Anderson coined for Latin America, the world is a "living museum."

Third and finally, many "modern states" are sadly lacking in many of the same "state-like" qualities that characterized the "sovereign" European states that evolved in the seventeenth and eighteenth centuries. Some old and other not-so-old states in the immediate spheres of influence of the superpowers face grave political, economic, and other constraints. They are scarcely independent entities. Moreover, it is no secret that many of the states spawned by decolonialization in the twentieth century are shaky enterprises indeed. In many cases, they are nominal rather than viable. The explosion in the number of states in the world has been striking. There were about fifteen such entities in 1871, twenty-five by the outbreak of World War I, and over thirty by the 1930s.[55] The vast expansion in numbers, of course, took place in the years following World War II. Fifty-one states were charter members of the United Nations, and the number of legally independent units looks to round out at well over three times that many within the foreseeable future. By almost any standard—size of territory, size of population, ethnic homogeneity, gross national product, degree of industrialization, military forces, forms of government, ideologies, and so on—these units present a wide range of differences. As David Vital argued some years ago:

> There is surely at least a *prima facie* case for asserting that one of the notable characteristics of the modern international scene is the growing disparity in human and material resources to be found where important categories of states are compared—with the result that the only genuine common denominator left is the purely *legal* equality of states that carries with it only such tenuous advantages as membership in the United Nations.[56]

And Oran Young is surely correct when he implicitly contrasts contemporary states with earlier examples as follows:

> If the basic attributes of statehood are taken to be such things as a clearly demarcated territorial base, a relatively stable population, more or less viable central institutions of government and external sovereignty, the contemporary

situation immediately begins to appear unclear and confusing.[57]

In truth, the common label of state masks more than it clarifies in contemporary political life.

The world is further complicated by the presence of an unspecified number (because there is no precise definition here either) of "microstates." This issue has been a nettlesome one for international organizations. For example, the League of Nations denied Liechtenstein membership on the grounds that "by reason of her limited area, small population, and her geographical position, she has chosen to depute to others some of the attributes of sovereignty" and "has no army" and, therefore, "could not discharge all the international obligations which would be imposed on her by the Covenant." Along with Liechtenstein, the League and the United Nations also refused to admit other microstates (or microsovereignties) like Andorra, Monaco, and San Marino. However, like the Vatican, they have held membership in various technical international organizations. In addition, Liechtenstein and San Marino have participated in the activities of the International Court of Justice, and Liechtenstein was even a party to the 1955 Nottebohm case on dual nationality (Liechtenstein vs. Guatemala).[58] Bruce Russett and Harvey Starr report that when Liechtenstein entered the Council of Europe in 1978, "a British representative warned, 'If we let Liechtenstein join, we may face similar demands from other microstates like Monaco, the Faroe Islands, Guernsey, San Marino and all sorts of others.' More importantly, some members warned that if such microunits were to apply, the Council might have to raise the whole question of what a state *is*!"[59] For theorists, no less than international organizations, these mice continue to roar.

THREE

The Search for an Ideal Type

The absence of a consensus regarding the attributes of a "true" state, as well as the historical origins of the phenomenon, suggest that we are dealing with a condition of *relative* political institutionalization, authority, power, and vulnerability across the millenia. Yet lacking such agreement about attributes may entail regarding virtually all relatively autonomous global subdivisions as variants of the state; the state then indeed becomes a "conceptual variable" and can no longer be used by scholars of international relations solely, or even usually, as an independent variable.

Under such conditions of indeterminacy the problem of constructing generalizable propositions of either a synchronic or diachronic sort becomes exceedingly difficult.[60] Contemporary comparison of state behavior is encumbered by the quite dramatic disparities in the units of analysis. Historical analyses of the sort attempted by projects like the Correlates of War (COW) are at least partly undermined also by gross differences—both across time and space—among the units defined as states.[61]

Is there an ideal type of state that can be used as a baseline for comparison with other variants of the state phenomenon— an entity that, on the one hand, is largely free from external control and, on the other, is distinct from its own society? Such an entity would not be a political subdivision of a larger entity,

27

and it would presumably be based on a different organizational principle from its own society as a whole. It would not be a "colony" or a "local government," or a "protectorate," as these connote relative dependence. Its institutions would symbolize the political community within its boundaries. Yet it would not be a tribal "chiefdom." Leaders and bureaucratic agents of "the state" would be readily recognizable as such, however "strong" or "weak" their capacity to control and mobilize human and material resources.[62]

The basic difficulty with such an approach is really twofold: First, even in hunter-gatherer groups and certainly in societies with a Big Man or chief, political decisions are made; the "authoritative allocation of values" process (as David Easton expressed it) does take place. There are differentiated political decisionmaking roles within the group, even though the same individuals may simultaneously occupy other social roles. There is usually little doubt about how (in the sense of a process and the individuals involved) an issue will be decided—for example, whether to move the tents to a different pasture, or whether to run from or fight a neighboring group. Moreover, most groups (even nomadic ones) have a defined territory or at least a "home range," and few of them are unclear about who is "we" and who is "they" in relationships with other groups.

Second, political entities are never entirely distinct or separate from their societies, because political decisionmakers do occupy social roles and must be responsive both to their own societies and to external influences. Indeed, as John Hall and others have stressed, the societies in which political entities are enmeshed, with regard to matters like defense or trade, typically extend far beyond their own "borders."[63] Political leaders interact differentially with *parts* of their own societies and the external world. Decisions of significance and considerable authority with regard to the allocation of values are regularly made at many different levels and through various social networks. Thus, if we are interested in explaining behavior, rather than in abstractions alone, we have to look both within and without the political entity in question. As we shall argue later, establishing that an entity is widely seen as "a state" may tell the analyst something relevant to the explanation of behavior, but it is normally far from all that is relevant and may even be the least illuminating explanation, or even misleading.

James N. Rosenau drives home the point about internal and external constraints in insisting "that present-day Beirut is the quintessential model for understanding politics." He says:

> Am I seriously asserting that the potential fragmentation of any system into sectors delineated by checkpoints at armed intersections is the underlying political reality? Yes, that is the message. Beirut is not an isolated example, driven by special forces associated with the unique history of the Middle East. Its tragedy is inherent in any political community and recognizing this . . . allows us to discuss and appreciate more fully both the fragility and self-reinforcing dynamics of political habits, norms, rules, and institutions as they are built up and sustained across time by processes of political socialization and learning.[64]

In Rosenau's view, delicate balances between different levels are, indeed, the essence of the universe that students of international relations must try to comprehend:

> The more the theorist comes to appreciate the relevance of these learning processes to the capacity of systems to persist and avoid collapse, the more she is likely to build micro as well as macro variables into her models and to see political life at all levels as sustained by individuals who are conditioned and constrained by institutions and cultures at the micro level even as their habitual actions also sustain these more encompassing institutions and cultures. This micro-macro interaction involves delicate balances that can be disturbed by either subsystemic or systemic developments, and it is the political consequences of these disturbances which often underlie the puzzles we seek to unravel.[65]

Consider one of the most (if not *the* most) intimate and integrated of all political entities in history, the Greek *polis*. In fact, even this term masks a significant element of pan-Hellenic identification, as well as a wide range of differences between and among individual city-states.[66] As M.I. Finley emphasizes, the label "city-state" is misleading, not least because it overlooks the rural population: "Athens, in the extent and quality of its urbanization, stood at one end of the·Greek spectrum together with a relatively small number of other states. At the other end were many which were not cities at all, though they all possessed civic centres." As for the Greeks themselves, they

> had no hesitation . . . in calling Sparta or Syracuse a *polis*,
> the latter even though it was ruled by tyrants during much of
> the classical period when 'tyrant' and *polis* had come to have
> virtually contradictory connotations. Nor did they deny the
> term to those backward regions in which political organization
> and the civilization itself were still so rudimentary that they
> were admittedly more like that of the *Illiad* than like their
> contemporaries. . . . And of course the word *polis* did not
> distinguish the structure of government; it implied nothing
> about democracy or oligarchy or even tyranny, no more than
> does "state."[67]

The Athenian view of the proper rules of conduct and proper
organization of social life was "radically different" from that of
Sparta. Moreover, "[w]ithin Athens—using that city-state as an
example—there was no single answer either, hence the long
complicated political debate which went on there."[68]

Not surprisingly, there were serious political tensions
internal to each *polis*, and these were aggravated by various
threats and pressures from outside. Since high civil and
military office was restricted to "men of birth and wealth"—the
policymaking "community" was actually a minority, excluding
all the women, slaves, and non-citizens. Finley describes the
tensions and contradictions that characterized the *polis*:

> The underlying trouble . . . was that the sense of community,
> strong as it was, clashed with . . . gross inequality. . . .
> Poverty was widespread, the material standard of life was low
> and there was a deep cleavage between the poor and the rich,
> as every Greek writer concerned with politics knew and said.
> This has been common enough in all history; what gave it an
> uncommon twist in Greece was the city-state, with its
> intimacy, its stress on the community and the freedom and
> dignity of the individual which went with membership. The
> citizen felt he had claims on the community, not merely
> obligations to it, and if the regime did not satisfy him he was
> not loath to do something about it—to get rid of it if he could.
> In consequence the dividing line between politics and sedition
> (*stasis* the Greeks called it) was a thin one in classical Greece,
> and often enough *stasis* grew into ruthless civil war. . . . [I]n
> the Greek polis it was not so much policy which caused the
> most serious divisions, but the question of who should rule,
> "the few" or "the many." And always the question was

complicated by external affairs, by war and imperial ambitions.[69]

Settlements in Greece to the east and west had perennial problems with marauding peoples like the Scythians and the Thracians, and the Persian and Macedonian "empires" at different stages presented almost overwhelming "external" threats. Yet, pan-Hellenic pride and cooperation in such matters as the Olympic Games and maintenance of shrines like Delphi notwithstanding, "external threat" in practice also often meant other Greeks. The Peloponnesian War among the Greeks, more than any other factor, eventually left them open to conquest by Macedon.

Historical "empires," too, had to confront any number of challenges from within and without. John H. Kautsky observes that the governments of "aristocratic empires" are, "measured by modern standards, extremely limited," not much more than "an internal revenue service and a war department." "Even the military protection from which villages and towns may benefit" is "a mere incident of intraaristocratic competition." Moreover, government is limited "because the peasant villages and, to a degree, those elements in the towns not directly tied to the aristocracy, form autonomous societies" that "govern themselves." In Kautsky's view, even "so-called centralized bureaucratic empires are, in fact, decentralized by modern standards." The central aristocracy has no alternative but to depend on local aristocrats to collect taxes, and "whether they are feudal lords or bureaucrats . . . they always retain as large a part of the taxes as possible and pass on . . . as small a part as possible." Such conditions produce centrifugal tendencies. "Provincial governors or satraps, like feudal lords, may then easily become or be tempted to become independent rulers in their own empires."[70]

S.N. Eisenstadt, in his seminal work, has much to say about bureaucracies, social groups, and external forces as they have had an impact upon the political systems of empires. He regards the bureaucracy as a "focal point in the political process in the historic bureaucratic societies," insofar as it was the "most important mechanism" by which a ruler might perform the critical task of responding to the demands of key groups in society at large and linking them to the center. Nevertheless, "the possibility grew that the bureaucracy's goals of service would be displaced by goals of self-aggrandizement, and so did the possibility that it would usurp power."[71] In addition, Eisenstadt notes, major changes in the political systems of historical bureaucratic societies came about through "some combination of external and internal pressures."[72] "Many [systems] were largely contingent upon fortuitous historical and external circumstances (e.g. population movements) outside the given polity," although the nature of the polity itself tended to determine both to which outside pressures it would be susceptible and the likely form of the changes that would ensue.[73]

What, then, of the "modern state," that ideal type which many scholars conveniently date in the West from the Treaty of Westphalia in 1648. Some scholars would suggest an earlier date—or, indeed, a later one—which is symptomatic of the problem. There is no more consensus about when and what "modern" connotes than there is about "autonomy" or the elusive state concept itself. James Anderson comments: "Whilst absolutist states look 'modern' when contrasted with medieval states, they appear very archaic when contrasted with later state forms."[74]   The question remains whether we have one "state" form with "medieval," "absolutist," and "modern" variations (or more: e.g., "early modern"); or political systems in different historical periods that are evolving into a "true" state; or political systems that are too different to put under a single concept.

Be that as it may, the circa-Westphalia "state" is credited, to some extent correctly, with having overcome the universalist pretensions of the Roman Church and the Holy Roman Empire, as well as the internal challenge of segmentary feudalism. Monarchs became "divine right," "absolute" "sovereigns," viewed as such from both inside and outside their domains, and the "state" itself took on the attribute—the key one for John H. Herz—of "territoriality" (a "hard shell" of "impenetrability").[75]

History has tended to caricature the status of the model sovereigns of the eighteenth century and to identify them with their realms. The "absolute" monarchs of Europe—those few whose realms were sufficiently integrated for them to claim the title—would have viewed their world as considerably more complex. In reality, they were repeatedly challenged at home and abroad, and their behavior was considerably more constrained than their "absolute" authority might imply. There always seemed to be a bastard "pretender" raising an army, or dissident nobles to curb, or rebellious towns and peasants from whom adequate taxes had to be extracted, with difficulty, to pay for a mercenary army to defend the "hard shell." A centralized bureaucracy was created, but more often than not the king's urgent need for cash meant that offices had to be sold to the highest aristocratic or even bourgeois bidder (and thence usually to be passed on in inheritance). And a monarch rarely knew if his nobles would answer his call for assistance when such assistance was vital.

Accordingly, one must agree with Roger King that the label "absolutism" is a "misnomer." In his estimation, "it did not involve untrammelled despotism, as the description implies, but rather claims to power. Absolutist states lacked the organizational capacity in the sixteenth and seventeenth centuries to clearly monopolize the means of violence within their boundaries, or to obtain the resources, or command the allegiance of their peoples, that would warrant [that] description."[76] Perry Anderson writes in a similar vein:

> No Absolutist State could ever dispose at will of the liberty or landed property of the nobility itself, or the bourgeoisie, in the fashion of the Asian tyrannies coeval with them. Nor did they ever achieve any complete administrative centralization or juridical unification; corporative particularisms and regional heterogeneities inherited from the mediaeval epoch marked the Anciens Régimes down to their ultimate overthrow. Absolute monarchy in the West was thus, in fact, always doubly limited: by the persistence of traditional political bodies below it and the presence of an overarching moral law above it.[77]

Kautsky, too, pictures the monarch as little more than one participant, albeit a significant one, in a complicated game of aristocratic politics:

> No matter how outstanding and even divine the monarch may be, he is not secure from aristocratic competitors who conspire to replace him. . . . [The monarch] needs counselors to advise him, court officials to help him run his extended household, . . . priests to legitimize his rule and his policies, military leaders to help him fight his wars, and bureaucrats to collect his taxes. . . . To become independent of some aristocrats and to control them, the ruler must depend on other aristocrats and may well be used or controlled by them. For all these

reasons, it seems appropriate to regard the ruler . . . with
his court simply as one more institutional participant in
intraaristocratic conflicts, along with other institutions, such
as the military, the bureaucracy, and the clergy.[78]

In fact, Kautsky points out, it is somewhat difficult to
distinguish these institutions one from the other, and the lines
of conflict often cut across them or subdivided them. Court,
military, bureaucracy, and clergy were themselves regularly
factionalized, thus opening up the likelihood of shifting
alliances among factions in different institutions.[79] Idealized
notions of a unitary state tend to disguise such characteristics.
They also encourage typologies that may not be entirely
appropriate.

Thus, John Hall argues, the traditional contrast between
the "strength" of absolutist France with the "weakness" of the
British state is probably "quite wrong";[80] nevertheless, one
should not therefore conclude that the British state was by any
means entirely stable and secure. Michael Mann's distinction
between the "despotic" and "infrastructural" dimensions of state
power is a helpful one,[81] and it does appear that the British
regime was paradoxically more successful than the French in
actually working its will on its society *precisely because* it was
somewhat less despotic. Hall remarks: "The British state had
greater infrastructural powers, being capable above all of
extracting really considerable sums in taxation. It seems as if it
is infrastructural capacity which really counts since the British
state proved itself superior to the French on every occasion bar
one in which they came into conflict in the period from Louis
XIV to Napoleon."[82]

However, Penry Williams in his recent and authoritative
analysis of Tudor rule, acknowledges that "the institutions of
government remained slender and inadequate,"[83] and that a
"review of the administrative machine and its resources does
not suggest that the Tudors had created a new and powerful
state." He explains:

[T]he men at the top were supported by only the most
rudimentary bureaucratic apparatus . . . the Secretaries
depended on their personal servants rather than a permanent
corps of royal bureaucrats. Intervention by government in the
social and economic life of the nation was seldom accompanied
by the creation of new executive posts and enforcement was

generally left to the existing officials, to local commissions, or to private enterprise. Nor was the bureaucracy well suited for the conduct of effective administration. Offices were held in plurality; meagre salaries tempted men to take gratuities and bribes; and payment by fees sparked off fierce demarcation disputes which often absorbed the energies of officials.[84]

According to Williams, what made Tudor rule successful (and he regards it as such) was primarily the Tudors' own "personal influence and relationships."[85] And, of course, only a few decades after the Tudor era came to an end in 1603 with the death of Elizabeth I, the realm was wracked by civil war, and Charles I faced the executioner.

Nor did the simple model of absolutism even reflect realities in the "model state" of Bourbon France.[86] Part of the "Sun King's" genius was his capacity to make life at the royal court of Versailles more attractive for his nobles than subversive activities back at the chateau.[87] The memory of Huguenots, Fronds, and other insurrectionists remained fresh. Had Louis XIV been a little less shrewd in adopting flamboyant architecture, dress, and furniture, his sun might soon have set. Moreover, he had to rule, in part, through his *intendents* and continue to be alert to clientele relations developing between them and various private interests.[88] So it is that Badie and Birnbaum comment that "not until the eighteenth century do we find Frenchmen beginning to think of France's borders as 'natural,' as later became commonplace."[89] Also, France was considerably less than a unified cultural community. Peter Worsley quotes Eugen Weber on the point that: "As late as 1863, 'French was a foreign language for a substantial number of Frenchmen, including about half the children who would reach adulthood in the last quarter of the century'."[90] Louis XIV ran headlong into the later-celebrated "balance of power" when he embarked on a campaign of conquest; his eventual defeat, in turn, may be regarded as both a ratification of the "hard shells" of some of his neighbors and as testimony to the rise of new "external" systemic constraint that had replaced the much less formidable Holy Roman Empire. Most significantly, a scant seventy-seven years after Louis XIV's death, the model state dissolved (or was fundamentally transformed) in Revolution, and the "sovereign" head of the "absolute" monarchy landed in the basket at the foot of the guillotine.

Scholars who cite Bourbon France as reflecting the

archetypal unitary state also tend conveniently to ignore the long process of decay that began even during Louis XIV's long reign. Robert G. Wesson's description of this is evocative:

> The model monarchy of Louis XIV decayed in its last decades, and some began calling for security of property and an end to religious persecution and arbitrary government. . . . Personal monarchy decayed into bureaucratic as government became professionalized. Roads, communications, and postal services that governments fostered for ease of administration and improvement of national economies, made for greater political awareness. New middle classes deriving wealth from nonofficial sources acquired more importance . . . and there was a revolutionary increase of foreign trade. . . . Growing knowledge of far off lands broadened horizons and assisted criticisms of domestic foibles. The idea that the wealth of the people made the greatness of the sovereign . . . grew into the thesis of "benevolent despotism," by which it became fashionable to think of princes ruling not by divine mandate, which lost intellectual respectability, but because enlightened, therefore benevolent despots were responsible for the progress and happiness of their people—a doctrine dangerous for monarchy. Although the philosophers saw no alternative to monarchy, recollection of medieval natural law gave a basis for new ideas of rights; and several thinkers derived sovereignty directly from the people. Power became a trust rather than a God-given privilege, a mandate to be exercised by reason. Contract theories of the state, a reflection of the importance of commercial relations, gained in importance.[91]

Overall, there are few examples where myth and reality diverge so dramatically as in the case of "absolutist" France.

Even if the absolutist myth had reflected reality, it would have been a very transitory reality indeed. The American and French revolutions had an impact on the basic units in the global system at least as significant as the emergence of the absolutist state in Europe. Earlier events in England had suggested the shape of things to come. As James Anderson observes:

> [T]he "Great Rebellion" of the 1640s did reverse the advance of absolutism and it shifted the balance of power away from the monarchy and aristocracy in favour of the commercialized gentry and merchants, and the realm of "civil society" in general. These changes survived the Restoration of Charles II

and they were confirmed by the abdication of James II in 1688—the so-called Glorious Revolution whose grandiose title masks the fact that it was actually much *less* important as a historical turning point than the upheavals of the civil war period.[92]

The doctrine that was gathering force held that "sovereignty" belonged not so much in a personal sense to a divinely-appointed monarch but, variously, to "the people," "the general will," "the law," and/or "the nation." That doctrine (however illusory it be judged) could legitimize authoritarianism or even rule by a monarch or a self-styled emperor (e.g., Napoleon I), as well as republican experiments, but it forever banished the notion that "sovereignty" necessarily implies the acceptance of a flesh-and-blood sovereign. In some measure, the changing meaning of sovereignty reflected empirical realities; it also, quite clearly, represented one of the most significant normative shifts in modern history.

Moreover, in line with Mann's distinction between despotic and infrastructural power, state bureaucracies and the state's impact on society seemed to grow even more readily when power at the center was exercised in the name of the entire body politic. Improvements in communications opened up new possibilities of control by government and the extension of governmental services into the hinterlands; continuing industrialization led to economic expansion, increased tax revenues, and an upsurge in international trade; while greater complexity in both the economy and "civil society" generated new demands for action by those in authority. The state concept acquired mythic proportions and became more of an object of popular identification and adulation. As a territorial unit, the state vastly expanded its physical size even as its surrogates expanded the scope and effectiveness of their policies.

In its several aspects, this was a state that might, with more justification, be called "modern." Yet it was also a state that was *itself* more complex and inevitably responsive to more complexity in both its internal and external environments. There was a much greater volume and variety of what Rosenau terms "micro" and "macro" influences on state behavior. The sources of state behavior thus became more difficult to identify and comprehend, and the intellectual cost of reification ever greater. If it was an oversimplification to think of the British state as "simply" Henry VIII or the French state as Louis XIV, how much more difficult it is to trace the roots of, say, the foreign policies of modern-day United States or Japan. On the other hand, one of the things that is particularly confusing for the contemporary analyst is that many of the so-called states in the world today are far from "modern" in the sense that we have been describing.

It was, of course, the concept of "nation," mutating into "nationalism" and "national self-determination"—the idea that each "nation" should have its own independent territorial "state"—that eventually had the greatest effect on global political boundaries. This essentially ethnocentric European idea was transmitted to the world, ironically, by the very European imperialisms whose continued survival depended upon keeping it from spreading. With the assistance of Napoleon's campaigns, two world wars in the twentieth century, the League of Nations and the United Nations, and the Cold War rivalry between the United States and the Soviet Union, a multitude of new "nation-states" have emerged.

Perhaps, as Gellner insists, one should not "conclude, erroneously, that nationalism is a contingent, artificial, ideological invention, which might not have happened, if only those damned busy-body interfering European thinkers, not content to leave well enough alone, had not concocted it and fatefully injected it into the bloodstream of otherwise viable political communities."[93] In fact, there are a variety of approaches to the idea of nationalism. For his part, Anthony D. Smith distinguishes three basic positions among scholars as to the significance of "nations": the "primordialists," who believe that nations are natural and universal; the "perennialists" (Smith's own perspective is closest to this group), who emphasize the antiquity and current relevance of collective cultural ties and sentiments, without necessarily asserting that such ties are natural and universal; and the "modernists" (like Gellner), who maintain that "nation" is best understood as a modern invention.[94] Smith argues, to us convincingly:

> [E]ven when we have subtracted many dubious "cases" of
> *ethnie* which turn out to be branches of other *ethnie*, or which
> were wrongly thought to constitute *ethnie* by chronicler or epic
> poet, we are still left with a very large number of genuine
> ethnic communities scattered across the globe and spread out
> through every epoch of human history. . . . [This] suggests
> that not only did many nations and nationalisms spring up on

the basis of preexisting *ethnie* and their ethnocentrisms, but that in order to forge a "nation" today, it is vital to create and crystallize ethnic components, the lack of which is likely to constitute a serious impediment to "nation-building."[95]

In modern times nationalism has provided an ideological justification for those who wanted to throw off the yoke of colonial repression and also, once legal independence was achieved, has provided an ideological justification for the leaders of new "nation-states" to rule. One can be charitable, with Gellner, and point out that the achievement of greater political centralization, the maintenance of political order, and the imposition of a "high culture" were essential if "Third World" countries were ever to "develop" in a world that was moving inexorably from agrarianism to industrialization. For Gellner, in fact, the imposition of a high culture was the most critical need: "At the base of the modern social order stands not the executioner but the professor. Not the guillotine, but the (aptly named) *doctorat d'état* is the main tool and symbol of state power. The monopoly of legitimate education is now more important, more central than is the monopoly of legitimate violence."[96] Or, one can stress, with Worsley, the persecution of dissident groups, ethnic and otherwise; the fact that nationalism has frequently degenerated into "chauvinism, from a pride in Self to a contempt for the Other," resulting in the extreme in "genocidal brutality."[97] Depending upon one's focus at a particular moment, both perspectives are of value.

Most analysts agree, however, that whatever relevance the basic concept of "nation" might have in some historical and other contexts, it is truly a "mystification" (Worsley's term) when applied to most of the contemporary "Third World." Gellner observes:

> It is nationalism which engenders nations, and not the other way round. Admittedly, nationalism uses the pre-existing, historically inherited proliferation of cultures or cultural wealth, though it uses them very selectively, and it most often transforms them radically. Dead languages can be revived, traditions invented, quite fictitious pristine purities restored. . . . The cultural shreds and patches used by nationalism are often arbitrary inventions. Any old shred or patch would have served as well.[98]

Worsley similarly believes that the state and nation concepts are natural companions:

> [I]t is more heuristically useful to restrict the term "nation" to that mode of ethnicity which only emerges with the modern centralized State, and which therefore entails not so much continuity with older ethnic identities as their supersession, if necessary, their repression. Nation-building . . . goes hand-in-hand with the formation of the State.[99]

In any event, nationalism is an ideology with proven power to inspire millions to acts of heroism and brutality. The "nation" may be an idea that defies easy operationalization, but it continues to exercise a powerful grip on the human imagination. An observer's understanding of the concept of "nation-state," which has dominated international relations discourse for two centuries, is basically ideological. This is typical of the subjective concepts that we utilize in international relations.

FOUR

The Many
Meanings of the State

In 1931, C.H. Titus conducted what he modestly called a "cursory examination" of various meanings of the term "state" and managed to identify no fewer than 145.[100] The reader will doubtless be relieved that the present authors have no intention of discussing nearly that many, but it is our intention to review some of the more prominent conceptions of the state that are to be found in the scholarly literature and elsewhere today. We have grouped these conceptions into three main categories:

1. Those that focus mainly on the state's relationship with its own society;
2. Those concerned primarily with the state's relationship with the international system; and
3. Those that view the state either as "Janus-faced" or as only one major "power network" among several.

As we shall see, these conceptions grow out of normative preferences and ideological predilections, and thus are entirely instrumental in character. They are fashioned less to achieve the conceptual consensus necessary for scientific investigation and theory-building than to advance normative and ideological goals. The categories, therefore, though convenient, are not theoretically significant. Indeed, it is not possible to focus on either the "internal" or "external" face of the state without implicitly or explicitly alluding to the other.

The State and Society

The state as a normative order

In this first conception, the state is envisioned as a symbol (or cluster of symbols) for a particular society and the laws, norms, and beliefs that both bind its people ("the nation" regardless of ethnic considerations) together and set them apart from other peoples in the world. In this perspective, a state has a juridical "sovereign" identity and status. Typical of this viewpoint is the observation of Alessandro Passerin d'Entreves: "The modern state is a legal system. The power it exercises is not mere force, but force applied in the name of, and in accordance with, a body of rules, from which in fact we infer that a State 'exists'. . . . [T]he birth of the modern state is no other than . . . the rise and final acceptance of the concept of sovereignty."[101]   The symbolic side of the equation is emphasized by Clifford Geertz, who has written persuasively about the symbolic role of the "theater state" in Bali, which he sees as highlighting a "pomp and ceremony" dimension common even to more complex states.[102] One is also reminded of the glorification of the state under National Socialism, or under other regimes like Getúlio Vargas's *O Estado Novo* in Brazil (1937–45).

In practice, virtually all states have their national flag, their national anthem, their leaders' frequent appeals to the mystical "national interest," their ideological banners, usually an Unknown Soldier or other martyrs, and the like. This state, then, is the *patrie* of the French Revolution and is a far cry, indeed, from the *État* of the Bourbon kings.

The conception of a state as a normative order, however, fails to address the painful reality that many countries, especially multi-cultural ones, are deeply divided over norms. The civil strife that today rends societies like Lebanon, South Africa, the Sudan, Peru, the Philippines, Burma, El Salvador, and even the Soviet Union is merely the most graphic manifestation of normative schisms. As the examples of the United States in the 1960s and the USSR in the 1980s illustrate, severe political turmoil lies closer to the surface almost everywhere than one might think. James Rosenau's argument, quoted earlier, that Beirut is not *all that* unique is surely correct. Aggravating internal divisions are normative conflicts sweeping across boundaries: divergent ethnic ties,

communism vs. capitalism or vs. catholicism (in Poland), Sunni
vs. Shiite Islam, and many others.

But what of the idea of "sovereignty"? In the late 1960s J.P.
Nettl declared:

> nowadays the problem of sovereignty is, for social scientists, a
> dead duck. More than thirty years ago, Frederick Watkins
> pushed sovereignty to the margin of political science concerns
> by insisting that it be regarded as a "limiting concept"—an
> ideal-typical situation that had to be qualified in all sorts of
> ways. He qualified it with the notion of autonomy, another
> limiting concept that applied both to the state itself and to all
> the associations within or below it, and as such eroded the
> value of sovereignty as a unique political factor. Since then we
> hear little of sovereignty except in the context of historical and
> philosophical (and, of course, legal) discussions.[103]

Nettl failed to foresee the situation today. For a "dead duck,"
"sovereignty" continues to generate a surprising amount of
quackery!

What do we mean by "sovereignty"? Theorists have been
working on *that* question for hundreds of years. One can easily
see the link to the state as a normative order in Hinsley's
definition—"the idea that there is a final and absolute authority
in the political community"[104] which legitimizes the decrees of
the state. Recall, for example, the very lengthy debate after
Bodin and Hobbes about where exactly in the system of
government "sovereignty" resided. In England, was it in the
Crown, Parliament, or where? In the United States, was it in
"the people," the Constitution, "the law" generally, Congress, the
president, or where? Theorists debated the question, but what
was really happening were struggles over authority. The
contest is still going on within countries: in the United States,
for example, among the president, various bureaucracies,
Congress, interest groups, political parties, voters, and others.
It also seems doubtful today that many citizens the world over
ever think about the "sovereignty" of the state as somehow
being the reason they pay taxes, serve in the military, or get a
marriage license. Partly for these reasons, the most useful
definition for contemporary times, in our view, is a narrower,
legal one, advanced by Alan James, that looks primarily
outward from the state—just constitutional independence.[105]
We shall return to this "external" dimension of sovereignty later

in our analysis.

The state as an ethno-cultural unit

Although scholars have generally maintained a distinction between "state" and "nation," the past century has witnessed an increasing identification of the two concepts at the popular level. Groups with self-conscious ethnic and cultural memories demand the legal autonomy associated with the idea of the sovereign state. In this context, the state is defined as an ethno-cultural unit. Commonly, this demand is justified by pointing to a common history or, if necessary, inventing one. By contrast, ethnic heterogeneity has been frequently cited as a source of state weakness and dissension (e.g., Austria-Hungary). Whether one refers to the unifications of Germany and Italy, the spread of the new imperialism, Hitler's campaign for *Lebensraum*, the founding of Israel, the partition of India, or the Nigerian civil war, the potency of this variant of the state is undeniable.

Indeed, it can be argued that it is this definition of the state—widely invoked by political leaders—that is largely responsible for the proliferation of ungovernable and unviable units in Asia and Africa.[106] Some states, through design or historical happenstance, are roughly conterminous with ethnic boundaries, but as we have noted, young states, especially, often reach for "shreds and patches" of past cultures in attempting to build a nation. In Worsley's words:

> The nightmare of the unifiers is . . . the realization that there is no logical limit on the size or number of groups which can legitimately claim to possess a common culture or subculture. The possibility of infinite regress opens up, for any sizable group can always be further decomposed into regional subcultures, each with its own distinctive territory, dialect, history, and so forth, and into further subdivisions within the region.[107]

It is precisely these fears that are repeatedly invoked in contemporary Africa against permitting boundary adjustments, however unreasonable existing frontiers may be from a tribal or national point of view. Some "extinct" "nations" have actually been reborn. The language of Hebrew, for instance, was virtually rediscovered as the Zionist cause was joined, and this development was integral to the rebirth of a Jewish nation. Worsley points out: "One of the most horrific cases of genocide known to history is the extermination of the Tasmanian aborigines. Everyone knows they were wiped out. . . . But what 'everybody knows' is wrong, for today there is a militant movement among the thousands who proudly trace their mixed, but nevertheless partly Tasmanian descent to their slaughtered forebears."[108] Some ethnicities, moreover, are much larger than many existing "nation-states"; Worsley's example is the 15 million Kurds stretching across Iran, Iraq, Turkey, and Syria—compared to small states like Dominica (pop. 80,000) or Nauru (8,000).[109]

Nor are the older and more established states immune to the "absent nation" phenomenon. For instance, W. Raymond Duncan emphasizes that in Latin America, where most state boundaries have been in place since the early nineteenth century: "[Indians] differentiate between highland and lowland Indians in Bolivia or village identities in Guatemala or Peru. Linguistic differentiation between Quechua, Aymara, and Guarani throughout the Andean countries also fragments the Indian community. . . . At least 73 languages are spoken [by Indian groupings in Latin America] and more than 355 separate tribes have been identified."[110] The United States has at least partially "melted" numerous ethnicities, but Black, Brown, and Red "underclass" tensions remain; ethnic divisions—most recently reflected in clashes between Armenians and Azerbaijanis—continue to threaten the Soviet conglomerate; Canada has to contend with its Québécois; Britain has the Scots and Irish as well as the Welsh; France, its Bretons and Corsicans; Spain, its Basques and Catalans; and so on.

Anthony Smith wraps up the situation neatly when he observes: "There is something of a paradox here. In theory, we require our societies to assume a single shape. In practice, we are content with a formal declaration of intent, while our societies assume all manner of shapes." He, too, highlights the fact that "there are actually very few genuine 'nation-states' today," and he provides some interesting particulars. If "nation-state" is taken to mean a single ethnic community and common culture, then only about ten percent of existing states would qualify. If some "tiny minorities" are left out of the calculation, a "few more" would qualify. According to Smith, this means that the probability of ethnic conflict is high indeed.

> [T]his leaves a very considerable number, perhaps over half, with serious ethnic divisions which may spill over into antagonism, and another large group, perhaps a quarter of the total, in which a dominant culture-community must accommodate the demands of "peripheral" *ethnie*, as in Britain, France and Canada, Romania and Bulgaria. In the 50 percent with serious cultural cleavages, it has not always been possible to contain the competing demands or meet the claims of rival communities. In India, Sri Lanka, Burma, the Philippines, Indonesia, Laos, Iran, Iraq, Turkey, Cyprus, Spain, Yugoslavia, Corsica (France), Ireland, Chad, Nigeria, Cameroons, Zaire, Zambia, Zimbabwe, South Africa, Uganda, Kenya, Sudan, and Ethiopia, these divisions have at one time or another since 1914 erupted into overt violence and even warfare.[111]

The state as a functional unit

Emile Durkheim, a leading proponent of the functional perspective on the state, reasoned that: "the greater the development of society, the greater the development of the state. The state takes on more and more functions and becomes increasingly involved in all other social functions, thereby centralizing and unifying them. Advances in centralization parallel advances in civilization."[112] In particular, according to Durkheim, the growth of the state goes hand-in-hand with a pattern of an increasing division of labor and specialization in a society. Sociologist Talcott Parsons's "cybernetic model" of this process stresses the differentiation of the political system from other social systems, which he sees as influenced by economic factors like the development of a market economy and critical cultural events like the Protestant Reformation.[113] For their part, Badie and Birnbaum describe this model of the state as follows: "[T]he state is one aspect of the rationalizing process that takes place in all societies undergoing modernization. State building therefore plays a part in what functionalists regard as the four central processes of modernization: differentiation, autonomization, universalization, and institutionalization."[114]

Badie and Birnbaum object, initially, however, to what they see as a neo-functionalist view of the nation-state as a "perfect

functional substitute for vanished community solidarities," an
aspect of the theory that shades off into the conception of the
state as a normative order. They observe that ". . . once the
state becomes an autonomous power center, with access to
previously unavailable sources of power, it becomes a target of
political action, an objective to be seized by every organized
group that wishes to impose its own ends on society as a whole.
The state thus tends not to quell conflict but to exacerbate it."[115]
In addition, the neo-functionalist model appears to confuse the
idea of state with that of a centralized political system.[116]
Finally, neo-functionalists seem to imply that "the state" is a
"universally valid political form suitable for all societies,"[117] a
position that, as we have seen earlier, poses virtually
insurmountable difficulties. In Badie and Birnbaum's view, the
crises experienced by political systems in Latin America, Africa,
and Asia stem primarily from an attempt to transfer historical
Western models to "radically different cultural traditions."[118]
Such efforts are basically ahistorical and fail to recognize the
advantages which a leisurely evolution of forms afforded the
Europeans.

> [T]he economic, social and political problems faced by third-
> world countries are utterly unlike the problems faced by
> European countries when states first emerged in Europe.
> Europe had to deal with a crisis of feudalism involving the
> private ownership of land by feudal lords. Most third-world
> societies, particularly in Africa, are currently faced by a quite
> different sort of crisis, involving the persistence of tribal
> structures, the crucial importance of kinship, and the limited
> individualization of property rights in land. Whereas
> European societies had to find ways to integrate already
> existing economic elites, the developing countries today need
> to create a market economy, to say nothing of a full-blown
> industrial society, from the ground up. Finally, whereas
> Renaissance Europe had only to contend with a gradual
> increase in the demand for popular participation, an increase
> more or less kept in check by organized civil society, today's
> newly independent societies have to face a much more
> dramatic rise in the desire for participation, which traditional
> allegiances by themselves cannot hold back.[119]

At this point, we should also recall two of our earlier
observations. Quite contrary to Parsons's view, we have argued
that political systems are never fundamentally differentiated

from their "own" society. Moreover, they typically are enmeshed with larger communities which extend far beyond "domestic" borders, so that it is extremely difficult, if not impossible, to establish precisely what a political entity's "own" society actually is. Much seems to depend on the issue and the way in which symbols are manipulated. For instance, the task of maintaining full employment in the United States today may be as much or more a function of the global economic system and the politics of international economic relations as it is of government policy in Washington, not to mention the domestic private sector. The international dimension is even more critical and visible in western Europe and certainly throughout the developing world. Neorealists like to picture governments acting jointly as functional managers of these larger societies, but it is far from clear who or what is managing whom, at what level(s) which values are being allocated, and with what degree of authority.

The state as a monopoly of legitimate violence within society

This definition of the state, in some respects a curiously atavistic one, was advanced by Max Weber. Weber's approach to the state is usually associated with his interest in the rise of a "rational" administrative bureaucracy and that presumably evolutionary process whereby a society eventually moves beyond the awarding of offices on the basis of patrimony and as sources of profit for the individuals involved.[120] Echoes of Weber may thus be found in Eric Nordlinger's brief for the relative autonomy of those groups of individuals who occupy decisionmaking roles in the modern democratic state[121] and also, with less emphasis on rational decisionmaking, in the governmental (bureaucratic) politics perspective that has become popular in the study of foreign policy.

Weber himself apparently recognized some of the deficiencies in his own generalizations about bureaucracy. He acknowledged that not all major "states" in history had evolved extensive bureaucracies and that even in Germany the bureaucracy had not achieved complete independence from the landed aristocracy.[122] As Held points out, Weber complicated matters still further by extending the notion of bureaucracy to "all forms of large-scale organization (the civil service, political parties, industrial enterprises, universities, etc.)." In the contemporary world, Weber believed, private and public administration were both becoming more and more bureaucratized, and the state was continually in danger of being victimized by private interests. One of his main concerns was "how can bureaucratic power be checked?"[123] Accordingly, his approach also shades off into an interest-group pluralist conception of the state. Finally, Weber stressed the state's role in maintaining order not only for the protection of property within its borders but also abroad, providing an umbrella of sorts for the advancement of citizens' economic interests in the broader international system. As a consequence, we can also discern links to a conception of the state at the domestic and international nexus.[124]

As for violence, surrogates of the state are, in reality, challenged from within *and* without. Weber's definition speaks not at all to the challenge of military or terrorist intervention from outside state boundaries. Nevertheless, the challenge from within is often even more serious. Many an elected Third World leader has found his arguments as to the illegitimacy of military coups singularly ineffective. It would also surely be difficult to imagine a Latin American or Asian president broadcasting Weber's ideas to guerrillas in the hills, convincing them to lay down their arms on the grounds that their violence is "illegitimate." In a sense, of course, that is what the governments of El Salvador, the Philippines, and Afghanistan do when they insist that they alone act for all El Salvadoreans, Filipinos, or Afghans—for El Salvador, the Philippines, and Afghanistan as a state. However, if there is no normative order, if there are no accepted ideological ground rules in a society, how can the exercise of violence by the government ever be truly legitimate? If there is no consensus as to whose violence is legitimate in El Salvador, the Philippines, or Afghanistan, does that mean that these entities are not states?

The state as a ruling class

Our next conception is what might be considered the traditional Marxist model of the state. Of course, in classical Marxism, once the capitalist class is replaced (as it must inevitably be) by a "dictatorship of the proletariat," the state itself will eventually "wither away." Paradoxically, the ultimate ruling class is thus not expected to have any ultimate interest in ruling! Be that as it may, as we have seen, Marx's own theoretical legacy was not entirely consistent in other respects and, partly for this reason, left considerable leeway for later interpretation. Marxists have subsequently taken full advantage of this room for maneuver. As Held notes: "Contemporary Marxism is in a state of flux. There are now as many differences between Marxists as between liberals or liberal democrats"; indeed, some Marxists have actually shown some affinity for the liberal democratic tradition regarding citizens' rights. Held explains: "The significance of 'citizenship rights' as a limit to the extension of state power has been more fully appreciated. At the same time, some liberal democrats have come to understand the limitations placed on political life by, among other things, massive concentrations of economic ownership and control."[125]

In fact, the normative dimension in Marxism has never been far from the surface; the commitment to particular ends is real, clear, and palpable. Witness Nicos Poulantzas's comments introducing his "theory of the state":

> The urgency behind this book derives above all from the political situation in Europe, since although the question of democratic socialism is far from being everywhere on the agenda, it is being posed in a number of European countries. The urgency also stems from the emergence of the new phenomenon of State authoritarianism, which affects virtually all of the so-called developed countries. Finally, it refers to the discussion of the State and power that is developing in France and elsewhere.[126]

For Poulantzas, then, theory evolves to serve contemporary social needs and must exhibit a relevance that is far more important than abstract "truth."

Present-day Marxist analysts differ as to the precise nature of the relationship between the state and the ruling class. Does a capitalist economic elite actually occupy governmental roles, or does it only influence decisionmakers (or some of both)? Does government always act as the ruling class desires, or may it occasionally act contrary to the immediate demands and needs of the ruling class so as to uphold the best long-range interests of the capitalist system as a whole? Stephen Krasner distinguishes in this regard between "instrumental" and "structural" Marxists.[127] However, as Held suggests, the difference between the two schools is often largely one of emphasis rather than substance.[128] For example, even while stressing the domination of the state by the capitalist class, Ralph Milibrand[129] does allow that the state must regularly rise above factional squabbles in that class in order to preserve the capitalist system as a whole. Poulantzas, emphasizing the need for state autonomy, nonetheless recognizes that the amount of autonomy the state actually acquires depends on a dynamic balance of social forces and that the state itself mirrors society at large by often being highly factionalized.[130]

The pluralist state

At the other pole from the classical Marxists regarding the nature of social groups influencing the state stands the early pluralist conception, associated primarily with the work of American political scientists Robert A. Dahl and David B. Truman in the 1950s[131]—the state as an arena for interest-group competition. In this model most significant interests in society at large are organized, and governmental policies are little more than a reflection of which interest groups, or "factions" in the Madisonian sense, are able to muster the most influence at any given time. Pluralist analysts and instrumental Marxists, as Krasner observes, both "view formal governmental institutions as relatively passive recipients of societal pressure." The difference is that for "Marxists, power is basically in the hands of a capitalist class; for pluralists, it may be exercised by individuals motivated by any interest that is salient enough to affect behavior."[132]

Neo-pluralist and corporatist models of the state

Occupying the middle ground between pluralists and Marxists regarding the relevance of social groups are these two additional conceptions of the state. Neo-pluralists like Charles E. Lindblom[133] recognize that interests within society at large are by no means all well-organized or possessed of adequate resources to place issues on the public agenda or to make their views effective in the governmental process. In addition, they contend that business interests have an inherent advantage in the competition, not only because of the extent of the resources normally available to business, but also because business welfare is fundamental to the very survival of the modern state (at least in the capitalist West).

Comparative politics specialists found the corporatist model, drawn from Iberian and Italian precedents, useful in characterizing the "new" military regimes that emerged in Latin America in the 1960s and 1970s, as well as the earlier regimes of Getúlio Vargas (Brazil) and Juan Perón (Argentina) and the Mexican one-party system.[134] It was observed that many groups were initially organized by government, that only a few were officially recognized as legitimate, and that those which were recognized tended to exist in a dependent relationship with government bureaucracies. Meanwhile, a so-called neo-corporatist approach has been applied by some scholars to the analysis of collaboration between government bureaucracies and interest groups in the making and implementing of public policies in Western Europe. In this view, government determines policies in close cooperation with particular interest group "partners," and policies are interpreted and implemented to a substantial extent through the interest groups themselves.[135]

Ruling elites

The elites approach is often associated with Marxist theory; however, one need not be a Marxist analyst to recognize at least the existence of an "establishment" of sorts in most societies. Charles W. Kegley and Eugene R. Wittkopf, for example, write of U.S. foreign policy: "In terms of background and experience, the people making up the foreign policy-making elite are strikingly homogeneous. . . . [T]op-level decision-makers are generally from the upper class and of WASP family origins, have been educated at the country's best schools and trained in law, and have extensive nongovernmental experience in major corporations and financial institutions."[136]

The work of Richard J. Barnet merits special attention in this context because it is characteristic of elites analysis and also because its normative impulse is unusually explicit. Barnet states in his *Roots of War*: "This analysis has grown out of a conviction that the United States has committed monumental crimes in Indochina and that these crimes are likely to be repeated unless we gain a much deeper understanding of what we have done as a nation and why we have done it." His "thesis is that war is a social institution, that America's permanent war can be explained primarily by looking at American society, and that America's wars will cease only if that society is changed." Barnet attempts to define "the elusive word 'we' so often invoked in state papers during the past generation."[137] He finds his explanations in a "governing class" with similar backgrounds, which controls a vast bureaucracy, maintains a "partnership" with business interests, and rules over a public that tolerates, and even to some extent supports, the kind of international adventurism Barnet deplores.

One of the perennial problems confronting the elites approach is how "elites" should be identified and the closely related question of the extent to which they should be seen as unified or fragmented. Thomas R. Dye complains with justification of "ideological disputation," "endless, unproductive debate," and a paucity of "operational definitions, testable hypotheses, and reliable data" that has long confined this field of study to "the level of speculation, anecdote, or polemics."[138] He concludes his own in-depth study of elites in the United States with the summary statement: "Our findings do not all fit neatly into either an hierarchical, elitist model of power, or a polyarchical, pluralist model of power. We find evidence of both hierarchy and polyarchy in the nation's elite structure."[139] The system is simply too complex, as Dye observes, for it to fit neatly into one or another of these models.

> Approximately 6,000 individuals in 7,000 positions exercise formal authority over institutions that control roughly half of the nation's resources in industry, finance, utilities, insurance, mass media, foundations, education, law, and civic and cultural affairs. This definition of the elite is fairly large numerically, yet these individuals constitute an extremely small percentage of the nation's total population—less than three-thousandths of 1 percent. . . . Perhaps the question of hierarchy or polyarchy depends upon whether one wants to emphasize numbers or percentages. To emphasize hierarchy, one can comment on the tiny *percentage* of the population that possesses such great authority. To emphasize polyarchy, one can comment on the fairly large *number* of individuals at the top of the nation's institutional structure; certainly there is

room for competition within so large a group.[140]

Elites theory, as Dye interprets it, "emphasizes underlying cohesion among elite groups, but still admits of some factionalism." One widely recognized "source of factionalism is the emergence of new sources of wealth and new 'self-made' individuals who do not fully share the prevailing values of established elites." These dissenters, who have been major contributors to the Reagan tide in recent years, Dye describes as "the Sunbelt cowboys."[141] In criticizing pluralist approaches, Dye emphasizes the very different processes that revolve around policymaking and implementation in the United States:

> The federal law-making process involves bargaining, competition, persuasion, and compromise, as generally set forth in "pluralist" political theory. But this interaction occurs after the agenda for policy-making has been established and the major directions of policy changes have already been determined. The decisions of proximate policy-makers are not unimportant, but they tend to center about the means rather than the ends of national policy.[142]

However, terming "decisions of proximate policy-makers" as "not unimportant" may be a serious understatement, not least because in actual policymaking means and ends often become so intertwined as to be virtually indistinguishable.

The state as governmental (bureaucratic) politics

This conception draws an analogy between the processes of state decisionmaking and an elaborate bargaining game among decisionmakers who are "players in positions." According to Graham T. Allison: "The governmental actor is neither a unitary agent nor a conglomerate of organizations, but rather is a number of individual players. . . . Players are men in jobs."[143] The governmental (bureaucratic) politics perspective suffered initially from some confusion because of its label, and Allison had to clarify the fact that it was not limited to bureaucracies but also included players in the legislative branch and in the political executive.

We will highlight only a few of the problems inherent in the governmental (bureaucratic) model, since this is obviously not the place for a detailed critique.[144] First, it is unclear to what degree the behavior of leading bureaucrats should be seen as institutional role performance, as personal behavior subject to idiosyncracies or cognitive perceptions/misperceptions, or as representation of clientele interests in society at large (pointing towards "pluralism" or "corporatism").

Whichever of these is more appropriate, it remains, in any event, extremely difficult to establish the precise identity of the governmental/bureaucratic "players" or to attribute behavior to bureaucratic interests. Policy is often made by a shifting set of ad hoc committees, and bureaucratic roles tend to overlap. In the United States, for example, the president's political appointments to top-level posts in the bureaucracy ensure at least a modicum of presidential control, even as the individuals concerned find themselves immediately counterpressured to represent their agency's concerns—including those of clientele interest groups—to the president and to cultivate a close working relationship with key committees and committee chairpersons in Congress. Bureaucratic divisions are further blurred by the fact that policy differences exist not only among various agencies but also within them (and within clientele interest groups like "business" or "farmers," as well), setting up the possibility (indeed, probability) of interagency and interclientele factional alliances. Congress, in particular, is so fragmented that it has no true spokesperson and rarely expresses through its votes anything approaching a genuine consensus.

Putting aside the difficulty of identifying the players, a third problem with the governmental (bureaucratic) approach has to do with the task of establishing the relative influence of the actors in the policymaking process. Is the president or chief executive regularly more influential than other actors? Or, does it depend on the perception that a "crisis" exists? Or, is the key factor the nature of the issue at hand, with some issues less likely to be in the political limelight and thus more easily subject to bureaucratic bargaining and control? At present, there are no clear answers to these key questions.

Finally, the governmental (bureaucratic) politics model, developed largely by U.S. scholars, bears distinct signs of ethnocentrism. The approach is unusually applicable to the

United States because of the constitutional separation of powers, the sheer size and diversity of the U.S. bureaucracy, the relative independence from the president that bureaucrats derive from their close ties with clientele interests and legislative committees, and the style of U.S. decisionmaking that allows for public debate and competition among different agencies. To be sure, the governments even of many developing countries are becoming increasingly bureaucratized. Nevertheless, the chief executives of other countries are not presidents of the United States; other national legislatures are hardly the United States Congress; and the style of bureaucratic behavior, including relations with clientele groups, varies tremendously from country to country. Kim Richard Nossal suggests, for example, that "in parliamentary systems the concentration of political authority in cabinet allows the political executive to impose constraints on legitimate conflict between policy-makers at lower levels in the decision making process." In consequence, the propensities of players "to engage in conflict to ensure that their preferences will be transformed into policy may be sharply reduced by the imposition of centralized authority."[145]

Stephen Krasner criticizes the governmental (bureaucratic) approach from a realist perspective and concludes that it is both descriptively and theoretically unsatisfactory. His most vigorous criticism, however, is reserved for what he believes is the hidden ethical implication of the approach, which, he believes, would encourage decisionmakers to mask their responsibility for choice. His conclusion is compelling, especially when he observes that foreign policy objectives are more a reflection of the values and beliefs of leaders than of bureaucratic competition. He continues:

> The failure of the American government to take decisive action in a number of critical areas reflects not so much the inertia of a large bureaucratic machine as a confusion over values which afflicts the society in general and its leaders in particular. It is, in such circumstances, too comforting to attribute failure to organizational inertia, although nothing could be more convenient for political leaders who, having either not formulated any policy or advocated bad policies, can blame their failures on the governmental structure.[146]

The statist view of the state

In fact, Krasner regards "the dominant conceptualization in the non-Marxist literature" to be the state as "a bureaucratic apparatus and institutionalized legal order in its totality." As he explains this characterization, the "final phrase is critical, for it distinguishes statist orientations from the bureaucratic politics approaches which have parcelled the state into little pieces, pieces that can be individually analyzed (where you stand depends on where you sit) and that float in a permissive environment (policies are a product of bargaining and compromise among bureaus)." Among other things, explains Krasner, "statist" analysts view "politics more as a problem of rule and control than . . . of allocation"; it is "not just about 'who gets what, when, how': it is a struggle of us against them." The state, in this interpretation, is "an actor in its own right as either an exogenous or an intervening variable" and "cannot be understood as a reflection of societal characteristics or preferences."[147]

Eric Nordlinger, whom Krasner classifies as a fellow "statist," nonetheless cautions that any "definition of the state must refer to individuals rather than to some other kinds of phenomena, such as 'institutional arrangements' or the legal-normative order." In his eyes, "a conception of the state that does not have individuals at its core could lead directly into the anthropomorphic and reification fallacies." Nordlinger characterizes his own conception as being somewhat "Weberian":

> all those individuals who occupy offices that authorize them,
> and them alone, to make and apply decisions that are binding
> upon any and all segments of society. Quite simply, the state
> is made up of and limited to those individuals who are
> endowed with society-wide decisionmaking authority.[148]

Nordlinger views *all* public officials as constituting the state apparatus:

> [T]he state should include more than the government and/or
> the bureaucratic agencies that derive their authority from it.
> Although the executive and/or the bureaucracy have been said
> to constitute the "core" of the state, this in itself does not

warrant a definition limited to them alone. Since we are concerned with all authoritative actions and all parts of the state as they relate to one another and to societal actors, the definition should include all public officials—elected and appointed, at high and low levels, at the center and the peripheries—who are involved in the making of public policy.[149]

Such a conception of the state invariably returns us once again to an old adversary, the problem of defining "autonomy." If the state is a conceptual variable, then it is impossible to say for certain what entity's autonomy we must attempt to weigh. On the other hand, if we cannot define autonomy, how then can we separate the state from other entities and influences that are not states but are said to constrain states? Can autonomy be merely symbolic, or must it mean a real capacity for independent decision and action? If a real capacity, must it be absolute or can it be relative? If relative, relative to what?

"The autonomy of any social entity," argues Nordlinger, "refers to the correspondence between its preferences and actions."[150] The social entity of particular interest to him is the "democratic state," which, we have seen, he defines essentially as all individuals (at all levels) who are public officials with the authority to make binding decisions, as distinct both from public employees without that authority and private officials.

Utilizing this definition, Nordlinger advances a "state-centered model," arguing that the autonomy of the democratic state has tended to be underestimated by observers. Part of the reason, he believes, is that too much emphasis has been placed upon cases where state and societal preferences have diverged. Equally significant, in his view, is the frequent convergence of state and societal preferences; and he stresses that, in such situations, state "preferences have at least as much explanatory importance as societal preferences."[151] (Query: Does it follow, then, that societal preferences have at least as much explanatory importance as state preferences?) Moreover, when state and societal preferences diverge, public officials have significant resources at their command to realign societal preferences with their own or even to act despite social preferences. Finally, according to Nordlinger: "Explanations based on societal groups dissuading American officials from making decisions they themselves prefer are undoubtedly valid in some instances, but not necessarily in most. More than likely, there are other important explanations having to do with the officials themselves being unable to agree upon what, if any, actions to take, what the most desirable and effective policies are thought to be." In fact, in the United States,

> [T]he sharing of dispersed power turns public officials into competitors for power, while their distinctive responsibilities help generate incompatible policy preferences. There is also reason to suppose that American officials subscribe to values and beliefs which do *not* place much store upon promptly adopted, coherent, positive, decisive authoritative actions to begin with. On either interpretation the state's preferences are fulfilled; it is acting autonomously.[152]

Nordlinger thus attempts to sidestep a major problem—the extent to which a state finds itself "constrained" by divisions of authority and policy disputes among its own decision-makers—by definitional legerdemain: The decisionmakers are inherently unified regardless of their differences because they collectively *are* "the state."[153] In the end, it is *only* a neat definitional trick.

The state as an executive

A more familiar approach is virtually to identify the state with a single leader. For all their limitations, absolute monarchs of the old regime would fit most comfortably into this conception (or thought that they did). Indeed, the law recognized monarchical ownership of both the persons and property in the realm. A few twentieth-century dictatorships would also appear to embody this notion of the state. The neon sign that loomed over the Santo Domingo harbor for many years read "Dios y Trujillo," accurately symbolizing, if not that the country was under God, that it was definitely indistinguishable from Trujillo. So, too, did the photograph of "Papa Doc" Duvalier that for many years was nailed to the front door of the cathedral in Port-Au-Prince suggest that the leader, church, and state were one.

This approach to the state contains within it something of the "great man" or at least key person perspective on history. In effect, one assumes that understanding the particular preferences and idiosyncrasies of identifiable leaders is sufficient to explain the policies of collectivities called states. It

is such an assumption, for example, that underlies Manfred
Wilhelmy's description of the foreign policy role of both Eduardo
Frei (democratically elected president) and Augusto Pinochet
(military dictator) in Chile as that of an *"animateur"* rather
than a "referee between contradictory positions."[154]

However appropriate the single-individual-as-actor concept
may occasionally be, especially in some traditional-society Third
World settings, it is obviously much more problematical as
applied to countries with complex bureaucracies and many
organized interests. Mikhail Gorbachev, for instance, seems to
be having a major impact on Soviet policies at home and abroad,
but he clearly cannot reorient them single-handedly. Most
governmental decisions are, in fact, made by groups, and the
idiosyncracies of individual leaders are tempered by role.
Leaders can be influential, but there is almost inevitably a great
deal more to the policymaking story.

The State and the International System

The state as a sovereign among sovereigns

Earlier we suggested that, in our view, the most useful
definition of sovereignty is the one advanced by Alan James
which looks primarily outward from the state, that is,
constitutional independence.

One must not underestimate the importance of a state's
possessing constitutional independence. As James points out, it
is usually a necessary (although not always sufficient) condition
for a state's participation in international organizations and
many other formal aspects of international life. Legally
independent states can lay claim to various widely recognized
rights under international law, including the right to legal
jurisdiction (not necessarily exclusive) over persons and
property within their borders and the right to send and receive
ambassadors; and with rights come such duties as not allowing
the state's territory to be used as a staging base for attack on
another state's homeland by its dissident groups.[155]

Also, in a very practical sense, legal sovereignty offers a
modest extra dimension of stability to states and freedom from
external interference that they would not otherwise possess. As
James notes, for example, there was much more of a controversy

over the Soviet Union's invasion of Hungary, Czechoslavakia, and Afghanistan than there would have been had these areas been a formal part of the USSR like Estonia, Latvia, and Lithuania. It is not insignificant that the Soviet leadership went to great pains to avoid the embarrassment of sending massive numbers of their own troops into Poland during the Solidarity crisis. For its part, the United States ran into much more criticism of its role in the 1954 overthrow of the Arbenz government in Guatemala, and for its armed interventions in the Dominican Republic in 1965 and Grenada in 1983 than ever would have occurred had any of the target countries been a state in the U.S. federal system.[156]

Robert Jackson has written eloquently[157] about the importance of the fact that so many states in Africa possess "juridical statehood" derived from a right of "self-determination"—what he calls "negative sovereignty"—"without yet possessing much in the way of empirical statehood disclosed by a capacity for effective and civil government"—what he calls "positive sovereignty." He remarks: "[A]part from a few qualified exceptions such as Morocco, Zanzibar, Swaziland, Lesotho, Botswana, Rwanda, and Burundi—sovereignty in Africa has never reverted to anything remotely resembling traditional states."[158] Most were "novel European creations" and are today what James Mayall terms "anachronistic" states or what others term "nascent," "quasi," or "pseudo" states.[159] Why, asks Jackson, are such flimsy states still in existence years after independence? He offers a number of explanations: "Once juridical statehood is acquired . . . diplomatic civilities are set in motion which support it, exaggerate it, and conceal its lack of real substance and value. A new international momentum is inaugurated."[160]

Many African (and other recent) states have themselves been too insecure to wish to see boundaries adjusted; the ideology of Pan-Africanism has frowned on regional states sitting in judgment on their neighbors, and what Jackson terms "racial sovereignty" forbids the rest of the world from criticizing the affairs of black African countries. Fledgling African states have gained status, information, and economic assistance from participation in regional and world international organizations; and, apart from rivalry over Angola and Ethiopia/Somalia, powerful external states have been largely reluctant to intervene extensively in African affairs. Most of all, Jackson argues, African ruling elites are doing very well, thank you—their countries are a mansion of great privilege for them, while the masses often starve. Jackson thus takes partial exception to J.D.B. Miller's assertion that sovereignty confers "vitality" on states; often "in Africa," Jackson observes, "it debilitates them and confers luxury on statesmen."[161]

So the legal concept of sovereignty tells us something about the "real" world, but it nevertheless speaks not at all to a great deal that is important about states and international politics. Start with the legal problem of how constitutional independence is established (although that is not the most important issue). There is no mechanism except the consensus—or lack thereof—of the international community. Let us leave aside technical problems regarding associated states and microstates. Consider the political passions that swirl around recognizing the sovereignty of the Turkish Republic of North Cyprus or the state of Israel. Or contemplate the fallout from apartheid: the "black homeland" entities like the Transkei that no state but South Africa recognizes. In contrast, "the former British territory of Lesotho, which is also an enclave within South Africa, but was never ruled by Pretoria and has gained independence from Britain, is a recognized state and enjoys full rights."[162] As these examples confirm, the status question is a highly variable one; an entity's "sovereignty" is highly dependent on external recognition (a contradiction in terms?), and some entities are "states" for some purposes but not for others. In some cases, sovereignty is conferred as a *post hoc* acknowledgement by the international community that a political entity is able to play an independent role on the world stage; in other cases, it is merely an honorific appellation that in no way alters a reality of impotence and dependence.

Neorealists tend to skip over the issue of how sovereignty is conferred and prefer to concentrate on its subsequent effects. Nevertheless, how to describe those effects has caused them no end of trouble. All tend to denigrate empirical tests of state autonomy. John Gerard Ruggie, for example, complains: "The concept of sovereignty is critical. Unfortunately, it has become utterly trivialized by recent usage . . . as a descriptive category expressing unit attributes, roughly synonymous with material autonomy."[163] Turning to what he calls "liberal writings on interdependence," he takes the present authors to task for having spoken some years ago of "the relative irrelevance of sovereignty" and a world wherein all "states are subject to diverse internal and external conditioning factors that induce and constrain their behavior" and some states are apparently "more 'sovereign' than others."[164]

Kenneth Waltz, another neorealist, is also troubled by limiting the meaning of sovereignty:

> The error lies in identifying the sovereignty of states with their ability to do as they wish. To say that states are sovereign is not to say that they can do as they want. Sovereign states may be hardpressed all around, constrained to act in ways they would like to avoid, and able to do hardly anything just as they would like to. The sovereignty of states has never entailed their insulation from the effects of other states' actions. To be sovereign and to be dependent are not contradictory conditions. Sovereign states have seldom led free and easy lives. What then is sovereignty? To say that a state is sovereign means that it decides for itself how it will cope with its internal and external problems.[165]

Ruggie is equally disturbed by Waltz's definition: "If sovereignty meant no more than this, then I would agree with Ernst Haas, who once declared categorically: 'I do not use the concept at all and see no need to'."[166] For Ruggie, in contrast, sovereignty "signifies a form of *legitimation* that pertains to a *system* of relations."[167] It sets up a world of "possessive individualist" states which interact largely on the basis of what Waltz calls an "exchange of considerations." According to Ruggie, domestic private property rights and state sovereignty are analogous. Consequently:

> [T]hose who would dispense with the concept of sovereignty . . . must first show why the idea of private property rights should not have been dispensed with long ago in the capitalist societies, where they are continuously invaded and interfered with by actions of the state. Yet we know that, at a minimum, the structure of private property rights will influence *when* the state intervenes; usually it will also affect *how* the state intervenes. If this concept still has utility domestically . . . then its international analogue ought, if anything, to be even more relevant. The reason for the continued significance of the concepts is that they are not simply descriptive categories. Rather, they are components of generative structures: they shape, condition, and constrain social behavior.[168]

But, the reader might argue, how effective is that shaping, conditioning, and constraining? In some states, for example in the United States, the concept of private property has greater currency than the concept of "sovereignty," and there is a traditional mistrust of "government"; yet government at all levels continues to impose a substantial tax burden, seize property through eminent domain, and the like. The fact is that the concepts of private property and sovereignty both pretend to a degree of "autonomy" which is often fictitious, and this, indeed, makes both concepts "relatively irrelevant."

A fundamental objection to focusing on the state as a sovereign entity is that it tells us much too little either about a state's autonomy from its society or from external impediments. Theoretical or legal sovereignty is often small solace to an entity facing severe constraints from within and without; it is by no means the same as having a viable government or economy or society or a unit that is significantly independent from others. All things considered, some actors *do* seem a great deal more sovereign than others and sovereignty itself appears relatively irrelevant as a guide to understanding actual behavior. Perhaps the concept's principal utility, which has endeared it to neorealists, is that it speaks to the legal framework of state participation in the international system and especially international organizations and "regimes." Politicians can use it in speeches opposing more involvement in transnational schemes. However, even politicians know at heart that participation in interdependence is not nearly as "voluntary" as the notion of sovereignty suggests, and we must look elsewhere for an explanation of why "states" do what they do in this regard. It is not enough to wave the tattered banner of "the national interest"; one must be able to specify the source of that "interest," why it is—or is perceived—as it is.

In light of the continued popularity of realist and neorealist versions of international politics,[169] it is worth reiterating something that many of us working in the field used to take almost for granted: Thinking about a world of sovereign states confuses more than it clarifies and certainly does not get us very far in theory-building. Indeed, sovereignty conceals as much as it reveals. In explaining behavior in international politics, there are almost always any number of more interesting and important things to say about almost any state than that it is sovereign! Hinsley acknowledges as much when he declares:

"Of some states, indeed, it has now to be accepted that they are sovereign even though they do not in fact rule effectively."[170] Granted that this is a technically true statement, is not the fact that a state cannot rule itself so significant that that state's formal legal status (although not insignificant) pales by comparison? James, "taking full account of the fact that the world at large regards the [South African] homelands as illegitimate and refuses to have any dealing with them," nevertheless places his emphasis on the fact that "certain defined territory . . . is now under the formal control of regimes which are constitutionally separate from that of South Africa."[171] Has he not got the cart before the horse? States find that other states, international regimes, nonstate actors like consortia of banks or multinational corporations seek to constrain their behavior and limit their autonomy—even as they (states) have an impact on all of them (other state and nonstate actors) in turn. For example, the international debt negotiations or international monetary matters generally involve a wide range of intrastate governmental actors, the IMF and various international lending institutions, and any number of nonstate private and semiprivate actors. Again, it is a contest both within and across the formal boundaries of states, and exploring the nature and dynamics of that contest is a primary task for us as theorists.

The state as an interdependent / dependent subsystem

If a political system is defined as a set of elements interacting with one another, then states may be viewed as consisting of one group of elements within that system with disproportionately high levels of interaction. Unfortunately, this notion of the state leads us directly into an ever greater conceptual muddle, for there is nothing approaching a consensus as to what constitutes the fundamental "structure" of the international system or the dynamics of change within it.[172]

For general systems theorists, what transpires in the international system is little more than a reflection of the whole, although there is hardly agreement as to the essential nature of the whole. A structural realist like Kenneth Waltz views the global distribution of power, especially the number of major powers, as the all-important system attribute. "Market structure," he writes, "is defined by counting firms; international political structure by counting states. In the counting, distinctions are made only according to capabilities."[173] Utilizing this perspective, Waltz concludes, for example, that the international security order is more stable in a bipolar than a multipolar world and that there is less economic interdependence under conditions of bipolarity. In striking contrast, a neo-Marxist like Immanuel Wallerstein sees the key system attribute to be the dominance of international capitalism, which, operating over many years, has divided the world into core, periphery, and semiperiphery with unequal development patterns. For him, the international system can best be understood as a "world-economy" that today is one of capitalist "hegemony," slowly being transformed by what he calls "anti-systemic" forces that one day (hopefully) will ensure the triumph of a benevolent socialism. The Soviet Union, in Wallerstein's view, was a charter antisystemic actor after the Revolution but has evolved into something of an establishment figure, itself challenged by such phenomena as national liberation movements and Eurocommunism. According to Wallerstein, the classical liberal consensus is gradually disappearing and also "schlerotic Marxism."[174]

In fact, what *really* underlies the gap between Waltz and Wallerstein in conceptualizing the international system and the states within it is a profound difference in normative commitment. Waltz sees a fundamental need for order; Wallerstein believes in the necessity of redistribution and change to bring about greater equity. Inequality is, in Waltz's eyes, advantageous because "great power gives its possessors a big stake in their system and the ability to act for its sake."[175] By contrast, Wallerstein argues: "The mark of the modern world is the imagination of its profiteers and the counter-assertiveness of the oppressed. Exploitation and the refusal to accept exploitation as either inevitable or just constitute the continuing antimony of the modern era. . . ."[176]

At the system level of analysis, regime theory has provided perhaps the most effective challenge to the dominance of the traditional emphasis on anarchy in international relations since earlier proponents of collective action were denounced as "idealists," and a realist discipline was imposed on a generation of scholars. For the most part, regime theorists have been able to avoid the wrath of the power theorists by accepting, in

Krasner's words, "the basic analytic assumptions of structural realist approaches, which posit an international system of functionally symmetrical, power-maximizing states in an anarchic environment."[177] The tightrope on which regime theorists sense they walk, however, is evident in Robert Keohane's observation:

> From a theoretical standpoint, regimes can be viewed as intermediate factors, or "intervening variables," between fundamental characteristics of world politics such as the international distribution of power on the one hand and the behavior of states and nonstate actors such as the multinational corporations on the other. . . . To understand the impact of regimes it is not necessary to posit idealism on the part of actors in world politics. On the contrary, the norms and rules of regimes can exert an effect on behavior even if they do not embody common ideals but are used by self-interested states and corporations engaging in a process of mutual readjustment.[178]

Most regime theorists follow Keohane's insistence that international regimes can function effectively only under selected conditions. Others, however, are prepared to go further, challenging frontally the classical assumption of anarchy by arguing that regimes exist in virtually all aspects of global politics such that there is order even in the absence of centralized authority: "[A] regime," Donald Puchala and Raymond Hopkins argue, "exists in *every* substantive issue-area in international relations where there is discernibly patterned behavior. Wherever there is regularity in behavior some kinds of principles, norms or rules must exist to account for it."[179] Although the latter view reveals a fearless disregard of the righteous indignation of realists and possibly scientists as well, it is probably the more useful one since it recognizes the universality and potency of norms.

Again, in regime theory, we confront a body of theory with a fuzzy concept at the center ("regime") that was propagated at least partly in response to policy and normative preferences; in this instance, the maintenance of order at the global level in an era of declining United States control, a preference which Susan Strange contrasts with the earlier interest in integration theory that "started with the perceived U.S. need for a reliable junior partner in Europe."[180] Although rarely explicitly acknowledged or explored analytically, regime theory has its antecedents not only in international law (usage, custom and norm-building generally) and functionalist and neo-functionalist work on regional "integration" but also in the growing interest in "transnationalism" and "interdependence" that marked the late 1960s and 1970s. In the wake of a period of détente between the superpowers and the frustrations of Vietnam, as well as in response to challenges like the perceived energy crisis, the dire warnings of the Club of Rome, and demands from the South for a New International Economic Order, attention in those decades shifted in large measure away from the familiar security issues like East-West competition and arms control toward economic and environmental issues that were presumed to be the leading challenges for the future.[181] The neorealism of the 1980s and its regimes variant, on the other hand, represented a step backward from the relative heady optimism of previous decades about the potential for international cooperation in these "new" issue-areas.

Influenced by the growth in the flow of transactions across national boundaries and other factors, many theorists in the 1970s and 1980s concluded that interdependence was intensifying.[182] But they disagreed about what the concept means. For example, Richard Rosecrance and his colleagues argued against too broad a meaning. "In a very loose and general sense," they declared, "one can say that inter-dependence is a state of affairs where what one nation does impinges directly upon other nations. In this most general sense, higher foreign trade, the ability to threaten atomic war, the development of worldwide inflation or recession all mean higher interdependence among states." However, this broad but vague conceptualization "is quite unsatisfactory for analytic purposes," embracing as it does everything from "fully cooperative" to "fully conflictful" relations among states—with the highest level of interdependence perhaps existing between "opponents in war," where "any improvement in one state's position would directly and adversely affect the other."[183] Instead, Rosecrance and his colleagues opt for a definition of the concept that excludes negative relations.

> "[I]nterdependence" [should be seen as] the direct and positive linkage of the interests of states such that when one state changes, the position of others is affected, *and in the same direction*. Interdependence, then, suggests a system in which

states tend to go up or down the ladder of international position (economic strength, power, welfare, access to information and/or technology) together. . . . Wherever interdependence is high, there should be high cooperation.[184]

By contrast, Robert Keohane and Joseph Nye, Jr. insisted that the concept of interdependence should not be limited to situations of "mutual benefit":

Where there are reciprocal (although not necessarily symmetrical) costly effects of transactions, there is interdependence. . . . [I]nterdependent relationships will always involve costs, since interdependence restricts autonomy; but it is impossible to specify *a priori* whether the benefits of a relationship will exceed the costs. This will depend on the values of the actors as well as on the nature of the relationship.[185]

They described two dimensions of interdependence— "sensitivity" or the responsiveness of one actor to events occurring in another, and "vulnerability" or the ability of an actor to insulate itself from events occurring elsewhere.[186] Their notion of interdependence, of course, is considerably broader than that of Rosecrance, and neither is preferable in any obvious way for theoretical reasons.

Clearly, discussions of interdependence are, as Waltz puts it, "confused by the use of dissimilar definitions."[187] Considering such divergences and the fog they produce, it is hardly surprising that observers disagree even about the level of economic interdependence that characterizes contemporary global politics. Rosecrance and his colleagues argue, for example, that in the contemporary world industrialized societies no longer stand to profit—as they did prior to 1914—from the operation of free market forces; American hegemony has been declining; the response of one economy to another has become less predictable; and the advantages that might be derived from greater multilateral cooperation have not been fully explored.[188] For his part, Stephen Cohen views the situation as one of "mutual dependency" arising from "the growing obsolescence of the nation-state as an entity capable of serving its people's economic needs."[189] Starting from significantly different assumptions, Keohane argues that international cooperation among advanced industrial countries "has probably been more extensive than international cooperation among major states during any period of comparable length in history," yet "cooperation remains scarce relative to discord because the rapid growth of international economic interdependence since 1945, and the increasing involvement of governments in the operation of modern capitalist economies, have created more points of potential friction."[190] By contrast, Waltz—preoccupied as always by great power politics and system stability, and striving to maintain a "pure" system-level perspective—concludes that contemporary interdependence is actually less than in the past.

> When I say that interdependence is tighter or looser I am saying something about the international system, with system-level characteristics defined by the situation of the great powers. In any international-political system, some of the major and minor states are closely interdependent; others are heavily dependent. The system, however, is tightly or loosely interdependent according to the relatively high or low dependence of the great powers. Interdependence is therefore looser now than it was before and between the two world wars of this century.[191]

Waltz's conclusion is perhaps to be expected because both his focus and his concerns set him apart.

As long as there are disagreements over the level of interdependence in global society, there will inevitably be disagreements over the nature and consequences of asymmetrical interdependence or dependency relationships as well.[192] There is, for example, little consensus as to the actual degree of "dependency" inherent in North-South relations.[193] Alberto van Klaveren, for instance, sees a loosening of dependency relations and argues that:

> Latin American countries are now adopting foreign policies that are increasingly autonomous from the hegemonic power in the region. Those societies continue to be characterized by a general situation of structural dependency, but the new realities of the international system and the relative autonomy of the state and its bureaucracy vis-à-vis the dominant classes allow for considerable independence in the field of foreign policy.[194]

It is rather paradoxical, but "independent" foreign policies pursued in recent years by the likes of Argentina, Brazil, Peru, and Mexico derive much of their support from nationalist resentments created by historical and continued United States influence in Latin America.

The *dependencia* perspective also fails to explore all the implications of the fact that the developing world accounts for a sizable percentage of developed-country markets, investments, and sources of supply.   Former United States Trade Representative William E. Brock estimated, for example, that the Mexican debt crisis alone resulted in the loss of roughly 240,000 jobs for the U.S. economy.[195] Argentine leaders, too, have become aware of the ability of the debtor to exploit the creditor. The Alfonsín government has been a hard bargainer in international debt negotiations, well aware that "if a country owes one billion, it's in trouble; if it owes 50 billion, the banks are in trouble."[196] Furthermore, the "pendulum" has swung, and "the initial incursions of multinational enterprise have been responded to with a reassertion of state prerogatives."[197]   To paraphrase Raymond Vernon, multinational corporations have themselves occasionally been "at bay" in host countries and nearly everywhere must contend with a web of restrictions on their investment strategies and day-to-day operations. Ultimately, it is difficult to determine the empirical merits of many of the arguments about dependency relations because they are so infused with ideological commitment.

Even were we to acknowledge that growing webs of transnational economic, informational, and technological flows are linking the fates of actors ever more tightly—a proposition that could be disputed by pointing to, among other things, the dispersion of new sources of influence, the explosion in the number of independent sovereignties and nonstate actors and the decline in American hegemony[198]—what would this tell us? Despite the best efforts of generations of theorists, we still really do not know something as basic as whether interdependence is related in any explanatory or predictive way to political cooperation or conflict.

A number of reasons account for the nonpredictive nature of analyses of interdependence. In the first place, the proliferation of transnational economic, political, military, social, cultural, and psychological ties on which much of the discussion of interdependence is based entails both potential benefits and costs. This is true even under conditions of asymmetrical interdependence; the relatively dependent actor will inevitably include groups that could reap benefits from efforts to change the status quo even while leaders may judge the collective impact of such an effort as harmful to the "national interest."

In the case of soaring energy prices that followed the oil boycott, for instance, Western banks stood to gain from the investment of recycled petrodollars; export industries acquired new markets for their products; and firms engaged in developing petroleum-substitutes were suddenly provided with new economic incentives. At the same time, consumers and groups vulnerable to the inflationary effects of oil price rises were harmed. Thus, Roy Licklider, in an empirical analysis of the impact of the oil boycott on the foreign policies of selected governments, suggests that "the oil weapon's effect on Middle East policy change was at best indirect"; whatever change took place in policy he ascribes to "the increase in wealth rather than, as the supply theory of economic sanctions would predict, the fear of future oil shortages."[199] Ultimately, judgments regarding relative costs and benefits will be based on incomplete or very murky information, and the final balance sheet will be at best crude, heavily influenced by subjective factors that condition perceptions.

That balance sheet is, moreover, importantly effected by countervailing currents in global politics. A growth in linkages among societies produces external pressures on governments in the form of potential costs and opportunities, while rising rates of participation at home create additional, often contradictory pressures, on political leaders from within. The increasingly participant nature of political cultures in both democratic and nondemocratic societies places severe constraints on the ability of formal decisionmakers to act autonomously. Under these conditions, the stability and even the survival of governments increasingly depend on their ability to satisfy a diversity of economic, ethnic, bureaucratic, linguistic, ideological, and other interests; and many of these groups perceive their interests as contrary to the external pressures imposed by the logic of interdependence.

In the developing world, the growth in political consciousness and localist militancy have created powerful countercurrents to external pressures, making it extremely difficult and dangerous for elites to capitulate (or be seen to capitulate) to these pressures. Popular antipathy toward the

IMF and the "banks," for instance, in a number of major debtor countries like Argentina, Brazil, Mexico, Nigeria, and Peru constantly threatens to contaminate continuing negotiations over debt. The intensification of local and sublocal "nationalisms" produces resistance to rising interdependence, repeatedly forcing local elites to act contrary to the logic of "national" or "global" interests produced by that interdependence. In addition, it is less possible than ever to coerce apparently "dependent" societies to conform to the norms of international regimes. Military intervention will probably produce massive local resistance; other forms of coercion will likely topple governments. In a word, "gunboat" diplomacy is effectively obsolete.

Nor have advanced societies escaped the consequences of this participation explosion. Its tremors were felt in the United States during the Vietnam War and are again being felt as intense pressures build in favor of protectionist policies that could erode international trading norms, and strategic policies that would in turn undermine the fragile arms control regime. In South Africa, Boer nationalism makes modification of the system of apartheid difficult for any government and produces resistance to external pressures for change. Similarly, in Israel, religious nationalism impedes resolution of Arab-Israeli differences, especially over the occupied territories; yet that nationalism is only exacerbated by foreign pressures.[200]

In Western Europe, too, the formerly protected character of policymaking in foreign and defense affairs is being challenged by social forces that threaten an Atlantic relationship that "serves the interests of so many states."[201] Until the late 1960s, the mutually profitable web of economic, political, and military arrangements was largely protected from domestic controversy by a tacit elite consensus regarding the necessity of maintaining cooperative Atlantic relations. Thereafter, the relative passivity of publics toward foreign and defense issues began to disappear, as greater accessibility to higher education and the increasing impact of the mass media familiarized and sensitized people, especially youth, to controversial issues such as Vietnam, nuclear power, environmental degradation, and nuclear arms.[202] Much of this came home to roost after 1978 during the debates over Enhanced Radiation Weapons ("neutron bombs") and Intermediate Nuclear Forces (INF). European leaders came to appreciate the difficulty of steering a safe course between the

Scylla of American pressure and the Charybdis of domestic protest.

The capacity of governments in developed societies to respond effectively to the logic of interdependence has been complicated by the proliferation of giant bureaucracies with close ties to specific constituencies. In the ebb and flow of bureaucratic conflict and competition that often accompanies political decisions in developed societies, individual bureaucrats and organizations are apt to represent the interests of their constituencies as well as their own organizational interests. To the extent that this takes place, decisions are further conditioned by internal pressures as opposed to external exigencies.[203]

Domestic exigencies and pressures, including those arising from bureaucracies, that push decisionmakers in several directions must be factored into any cost-benefit equation. As we have suggested, these may well outweigh pressures imposed by the apparent consequences of international interdependencies. In the case of the 1973 oil embargo, for instance, the Arab effort to force developed societies to change their policies toward Israel enjoyed only modest success. A principal reason that such pressure does not succeed, according to Licklider, is that: "National independence is more important to most people than economic well-being; any government appearing to trade the former for the latter is vulnerable to attacks on its wisdom and motives by its domestic political opponents. Thus, on balance, public external coercion can make it harder, not easier, for a target government to comply."[204] When internal conditions make it impossible for governments to respond "rationally" to the costs liable to be imposed by violating the norms of an international regime or by severing ties, it may almost seem as though decisionmaking is autistic.

Levels of interdependence, then, tell the observer little of a predictive nature, nor is interdependence adequate to explain behavior. Indeed, the fact of proliferating international linkages tells us little more than that life appears increasingly complex and confusing to decisional elites. Ultimately, those elites must determine the relative balance of potential costs and benefits they are confronting on the basis of very incomplete information that is perceived through lenses colored by psychological and political needs. Additionally, their evaluations of the impact of interdependence will likely vary by issue-area, often with only a rudimentary appreciation of possible linkages among them. On some occasions, leaders will fail to see important linkages where they exist (as did Lyndon Johnson in the relationship between the Vietnam War and global inflation). On other occasions, they may create linkages that previously did not exist in order to justify their behavior.

Many factors are likely to contribute in shaping the perceptions of decisionmakers about the nature of linkages and the relative costs and benefits imposed by interdependence/dependence. Among these are subjective definitions, political obligations, ideology, memories (individual and organizational), and personality attributes. Apparently objective indicators like transaction flows and the availability of alternatives (which may not be objective at all) may encourage the theorist to advise the decisionmaker that he ought to feel interdependent or dependent or run the risk of dire consequences for himself and those for whom he is a surrogate. And, in the end, even if there is consensus among decisionmakers as to probable costs associated with severing ties or the availability of substitute partners, actors will vary dramatically in terms of the price they are willing to pay for principle.

Janus state or power network

To this point, we have reviewed various conceptions of the state—focusing primarily *either* "within" or "without"—on the state's relationship to its own society *or* to the international system. Our final two conceptions self-consciously bridge what also seems to us to be this highly artificial, and even gravely misleading, internal/external or domestic/international gap. In doing so, they vastly increase the variables potentially affecting "state" institutions and policies, and so greatly complicate the task of analysts who must order such variables into meaningful theory.

James N. Rosenau pioneered the related concepts of domestic/international "linkages,"[205] "penetrated" societies,[206] "issue-areas,"[207] and states as "adaptive" entities (adapting simultaneously to internal and external environments).[208] The present authors over a decade ago characterized "world politics" as a "web" linking state and nonstate actors (e.g., local interest groups and international organizations) which were variously engaged in particular issues, and we used the term "Janus face" in a chapter title to describe patterns of conflict in Latin America.[209]

Most recently, however, the "Janus-faced" concept of the state has been associated with Theda Skocpol, whose initial work centered on the great social revolutions of history in France, Russia, and China.[210] Skocpol views the state as a "set of administrative, policing, and military organizations headed, and more or less well coordinated by, an executive authority."[211] The state is "Janus-faced" because it is linked on one side in complicated ways with "class-divided socioeconomic structures" and on the other with an equally complex international system.[212] As David Held explains it:

> Such a perspectivae helps illuminate: the way state organizations themselves vary; how the capacities of state organizations change in relation to the organization and interest of socio-economic groups and the "transnational" environment; how state personnel develop interests in internal security, policy formulation, and competition with other nation-states which may be at variance with the interests of other social groups or classes. It allows, Skocpol argues, the distinctiveness and histories of particular state agencies to be unpacked, thus "bringing the state back in" to the abstract theory of the state.[213]

Each state, in Skocpol's perspective, has its own distinctive history, its own identifiable structure and complex network of internal and external socioeconomic relationships that can and often do change over time. Each state, then, tends to be "different" from others in crucially important ways.

As sophisticated and persuasive as Skocpol's perspective is in many respects, it seems to us almost by definition to have limited utility for generalization and theory-building. We agree with Held that it is "less a theory and more a framework for the analysis of the state."[214] The very strength of the approach lies in its emphasis on the fact that each state *is* distinctive. There are obviously any number of potentially relevant variables at each level-of-analysis, and there may even be more if one is less sanguine than Skocpol, not only about class being the organizing principle of domestic society, but also about the executive's capacity to "coordinate" the state's "set of administrative, policing, and military organizations." Her contention that they are "more or less well coordinated" appears to fudge over what we have seen to be a major analytical problem.

Skocpol continues to finesse this and other critical issues in her later work. She gives "respectful attention" to "doubts about the superior rationality of state actions," but asserts that "we need not entirely dismiss the possibility that partially or fully autonomous state actions *may* [emphasis in the original] be able to address problems and even find 'solutions' beyond the reach of societal actors and those parts of government closely constrained by them." As she assesses it: "[A]utonomous official initiatives can be stupid or misdirected, and autonomous initiatives may be fragmented and partial and work at cross-purposes to one another. Notwithstanding all of these possibilities, however, state initiatives may sometimes be coherent and appropriate." We are struck by the repeated use of the verb "may" and need to know under what circumstances "sometimes" is applicable. Consider also Skocpol's reflections on the fact that "autonomous state activity . . . can never really be 'disinterested' in any meaningful sense":

> This is true not only because all state actions necessarily benefit some social interests and disadvantage others. . . . More to the point, autonomous state actions will regularly take forms that attempt to reinforce the authority, political longevity, and social control of the state organizations whose incumbents generated the relevant policies or policy ideas. . . . Whether rational policies result may depend on how "rational" is defined and might even be largely accidental. The point is that policies different from those demanded by societal actors will be produced. The most basic research task for those interested in state autonomy surely is to explore why, when, and how such distinctive policies are fashioned by states.[215]

Hence we are back to square one, and there is obviously an excellent reason for all the "mays."

Clouding the matter even more are linkages among societies, as Skocpol and her fellow editors also remind us:

> Analysts must take account of the embeddedness of nations in changing transnational relations, such as wars and interstate alliances or balances of power, market flows and the international division of labor, and patterns of intellectual communication or cultural modeling across national

boundaries. Since states are intrinsically Janus-faced,
standing at the intersections of transnational and domestic
processes, their structures, capacities, and policies are always
influenced by identifiable aspects of the particular world
historical circumstances in which they exist.[216]

So how can any state ever be "autonomous" in any clear
sense, and where in the midst of all these lists of possible
influences on state behavior is there any firm basis for
generalization? Skocpol and company highlight some important
relationships that should by now be becoming painfully familiar
to the reader, but really tell the observer little except that he
needs to know more. It may then be that "bringing the state
back in" produces the departure of general theory.

Michael Mann opens the Pandora's box of potentially
relevant variables still further by suggesting that the state
should be conceived as only one of several power networks. He
derives his "provisional working definition" of "the state" from
Weber: "The state is a differentiated set of institutions and
personnel embodying centrality, in the sense that political
relations radiate outward to cover a territorial demarcated area,
over which it claims a monopoly of binding and permanent rule-
making, backed up by physical violence."[217] That *definition* is
much less exceptional than Mann's *conception* of the state, as
enmeshed in a much wider "social" context. This derives, not
from Weber, but from Mann's own insistence that we should
abandon the notion of a unitary "society." "Human beings," he
argues, are "social, not societal." "Social relationships have
rarely aggregated into unitary societies," however much some
states may have had "unitary pretensions." Societies are
"organized," "confederal, overlapping, intersecting networks"
rather than "simple totalities"; and social institutions draw to
varying degrees (in a "promiscuous" fashion) upon four major
sources of social power (ideological, economic, military, and
political).

The primacy of institutions rests, ultimately, upon their
relative capacity to satisfy human goals. Writes Mann:
"Organizations and functions weave across each other in the
historical process, now separating clearly, now merging in
varying forms. Economic roles can be (and normally are)
performed by states, by armies, and by churches, as well as by
specialized organizations we generally call 'economic.'
Ideologies are brandished by economic classes, by states, and by

military elites, as well as by churches and the like. There are no one-to-one relations between functions and organizations." Mann acknowledges that in its broadest sense "political power," too, may be exercised by almost any organization, although he prefers to confine it to "regulations and coercion centrally administered and territorially bounded—that is, to *state* power." States get whatever primacy they may (or may not) enjoy from "the usefulness of centralized, institutionalized, territorialized regulation of many aspects of social relations." As Mann defines it, "political power heightens boundaries, whereas the other power sources may transcend them." Moreover, overarching states' territorial boundaries, he recognizes the existence of a pattern of "geopolitical organization" that is also "an essential part of social life" and "is not reducible to the 'internal' power configurations of its component states."[218]

Mann's conception of the state as one power network among several is provocative, and his effort to generate various analytical categories (e.g., the four main sources of social power) makes his work less diffuse than it might otherwise be. He wisely observes: "Societies are much *messier* than our theories of them."[219] Thus he might argue that his framework, if anything, is not diffuse enough to capture fully what is actually happening! Nonetheless, as he himself suggests, the task of organizing such an array of social relationships into coherent theory is, indeed, a formidable one. We look forward to volume three of his trilogy, wherein he proposes to advance his overall theoretical conclusions.

Several additional observations might be made at this stage. In our view, Mann's conception is of considerable value, because it explicitly regards the state as being in competition with other power networks for a share of human resources and loyalties. The state may not always be the primary focus of identification, and even when it is, it is never the only symbol of identification. Whatever authority states enjoy is always tentative; it varies over time. Moreover, not all states allocate the same range of values. Another strength of Mann's approach is that it is historically grounded: His first two volumes are mostly historical (and prehistorical) case studies, beginning before the emergence of "civilization" in Mesopotamia.

His insights notwithstanding, some fundamental issues remain regarding Mann's work. Why restrict the notion of political power to "state" power, and, yes, what is a "state" anyway? Behind the Weberian prose and the power center label, what sort of real identity and autonomy are there? Mann maintains that "political relations concern one particular area, the 'center'." That is patently inaccurate even in a "modern" state context like that in the United States today, where fifty states and thousands of localities—not to mention political parties, interest groups, bureaucracies, and countless individuals—are constantly engaged in a struggle over, and the exercise of, genuine political power. Are most states a single power network or many? Are they, unlike societies, a unitary actor? Mann's preoccupation with "states" leads him into another difficulty on the "external" side: If political power is to be limited to "centrally administered and territorially bounded" state power, how can it come into play in the "international" arena? The best he can do is to posit "an area of regulated interstate relations." Yet he admits that the relationships and institutions that result are more than the sum of state parts and, in somewhat contradictory fashion, goes so far as to characterize "geopolitical diplomacy" as "a second important form of political-power organization."[220] The perennial questions return: How shall "international relations" be conceived? How autonomous are states, and how do other power networks figure in this broader political context?

FIVE

The State, Conceptual Chaos, and the Future of International Relations Theory

The many meanings of "the state" we have reviewed—and of course we might have considered still others—leave us with almost no meaning at all. We do not have one state or many states—we essentially have none. "The state" has little substance as an empirical concept and virtually no utility as an analytic concept; it obscures far more than it clarifies. If we are interested in explaining behavior—and surely that is what we as students of international relations are all about, absent the methodological trappings of "behaviorism"—the state concept only muddies the waters. Except in strictly normative and narrowly legal terms, "states" do not act ("behave") and, even to the extent that they do in normative and legal terms, explaining *why* they act as they do—why state policies are what they are, for example—requires us to look elsewhere. *In particular cases,* individual leaders act, bureaucracies act, ruling elites act, "regimes" act, and so on, but states do not, except insofar as we deceive ourselves into thinking of them as sovereign billiard balls bumping into each other on a world as flat as a billiard table.

If the state is such a failed concept, why, one wonders, does it continue to occupy such a prominent place in the minds of ordinary citizens and international relations scholars? We do not wish to overstate a case for the sake of argument: The state does have *some* empirical content. It continues today to be the

81

primary normative symbol of identification for many of the world's inhabitants, although it is easy, especially for citizens in the West (including most international relations theorists), vastly to underestimate the attraction and policy impact of other symbols. (To what extent have Khomeini's frenzied hordes been dying for Iran or for their own fundamentalist version of Islam?) Nevertheless, when all is said and done, the state remains a powerful symbol. And, as James reminds us and we have discussed at length, the legal notion of sovereignty does have *some* practical consequences in the international arena.

However, international relations scholars have an additional, not entirely rational, reason for clinging to the state concept. Like a well-worn teddy bear, the state is a familiar comfort to them in the midst of encircling night. So many of us are, in an intellectual rather than political sense, basically conservative. This would be fine if only we had something truly worth conserving. We can talk about the need for parsimony in our theoretical constructs, but, underneath, the truth is that we hate to give up an old realist myth. We refuse to acknowledge how little it actually informs us; how little we consequently know. We are thus militantly ignorant and wilfully deny ourselves the beginning of wisdom. T.S. Eliot might have been thinking of us when he wrote that we humans "cannot bear very much reality" (no pun intended).

Whether we are ready to face it or not, the reality implicit in conceptual chaos is that international relations is barely a "field" and is certainly not a discipline. As we have argued before, one must have a firm idea of "the state" in order to infer what is "interstate" or "international." A discipline that cannot agree on the meaning of such a central concept is obviously in serious straits, and one might understandably have grave doubts about its future. Unfortunately, as we also stressed at the outset, the state is definitely not the only troublesome concept in international relations. Most of the others we use are also intolerably fuzzy or "soft." "Autonomy," "aggression," "imperialism," "interdependence," "dependency," "regime," and many others continue to have any number of different connotations. It is not simply that there have been multiple meanings from an historical perspective, but that there is no greater consensus today than in the past. This is especially disappointing in light of the professed dedication of two generations of scholars to transform international relations into a science.

The problem of the state concept is, at root, symptomatic of a more profound analytical muddle across the entire international relations field. International relations scholarship is repeatedly hampered not only by its failure to achieve consensus in regards to *individual* concepts but also by its inability to generate a *stable* of consensual concepts. The sad truth is that this may be a virtually impossible task owing to the contextual nature of perceptions and to shifts in the values of societies in which scholarship is conducted.

Ultimately, unique concepts are the bases of disciplinary boundaries and are prerequisites to identifying a common set of problems and puzzles that constitute the *raisons d'être* of its practitioners. In the absence of such boundaries, it is not even clear who is in a field and who is not. The moral theologian, the psychiatrist, the agricultural specialist, and many others may equally and plausibly claim to be involved in international relations research. And, in the absence of conceptual rigor and relatively clear boundaries, individual scholars or groups of scholars will continue to pursue idiosyncratic lines of research, often in isolation from one another. They will continue to contemplate different, even unrelated, problems or, what is even more frustrating, may genuinely believe that they are addressing the same problem, only to discover (or fail to discover) that this is not the case.

What we face in international relations is not simply the problem of disciplinary immaturity; and its solution is not to be found in forcing conceptual consensus upon an unwilling and fractious community of scholars. The absence of such consensus cannot be explained merely as a consequence of the abstract and inherently complex nature of the phenomena with which we deal (although this is obviously part of the problem). There are more fundamental reasons for repeated quarrels over the meaning of key concepts:

- The power to define affords the power to control;
- Concepts in the social sciences are inherently value-laden and reflect the normative biases of theorists;
- Theory and practice are inseparable aspects of a single enterprise.

Key concepts in the field serve as potent political and psychological symbols for scholars and practitioners. Social scientists are, as a rule, less "objective" in their search for definitions of phenomena than they care to admit or may even realize. Instead, definitions are shaped to conform to value preferences that are rarely articulated and serve as weapons in the battles waged among intellectual protagonists. At stake in these battles are government support, offices in academic associations, promotions and merit awards, and, in general, disciplinary prestige. For policymakers, on the other hand, control of concepts is a source of unique authority and legitimacy. This is the "1984" function of definitions. Decisions regarding definitions, then, may actually *follow* analysis, rather than preceding it as we commonly assume.

The second and perhaps more fundamental problem that precludes consensus as to the meaning of social science phenomena like the state is that they are inherently value-laden. Even in the same era, scholars and practitioners will differ markedly in their conceptualizations. Their varying definitions will reflect distinctive ideological and contextual predispositions regarding threats to value satisfaction.

Finally, social science concepts are forged with an eye on practical politics, and scholars cannot isolate themselves from the milieu in which they seek to address issues. Therefore, unlike the natural sciences, the social sciences *only* have meaning within a social context. Theory and practice are like Siamese twins and can be separated, if at all, only at enormous cost to both. Were social scientists somehow able to develop a consensual body of concepts, that very triumph would serve to render their work even more irrelevant to practitioners whose ideas must be forged and tested in a very real sociopolitical context.

Our concern, then, is not merely that the field is characterized by intellectual disturbance—for a degree of controversy can also be a sign of life—or that, as Dina Zinnes notes, "the literature has not been very helpful in identifying the unit of analysis."[221] More importantly, we believe that the concepts which bedevil us are inseparable from the norms, ideologies, political aspirations, and personal biases that animate the scholars and practitioners in our field. If this is so, then concepts like the state can never assume the objective and operational qualities that are prerequisites to scientific observation and analysis. They will also continue to plague theory-building along any methodological lines.

As a consequence of the heavy normative content of the concepts in international relations, many, if not most, of basically the same theoretical arguments and emphases tend to reappear over and over again through time despite apparent changes in concepts and discourse. Behind them lurk enduring normative themes like realism and idealism or anarchy and order. Each theoretical perspective draws its inspiration from partial views of a world that, despite genuine evolution and critical events, is not changing nearly as much as shifting theoretical fashions and the rhetoric of scholarly contest might appear to suggest.

Where can we in the international relations field possibly go from here? The present authors have a few suggestions, although it would hardly be consistent of us not to acknowledge readily their subjective character. One understandable reaction to conceptual chaos might be to throw up one's hands and utter a long plaintive howl of despair. That might make one feel a little better; in fact, there is what we hope is a dignified sort of howl between the lines of this book. Obviously, though, most of us are too interested in the subject of international relations (whatever that is) to give up studying it as systematically as possible. How, then, might we proceed?

First, let us recognize from the start that the field of international relations will inevitably have to resemble the humanities much more than the natural sciences. We are not a "science," although some of our concerns are "social." The scientific revolution in the field, for the time being at least, appears to be a deader duck even than Nettl's sovereignty. Our analysis of the state and other key concepts in international relations strongly suggests that their inherent subjectivity does more than inhibit cumulative research in the conventional scientific sense; it probably defeats the enterprise at the outset. Many, if not most, of the concepts we use do not serve as building-blocks for theory but are obstacles to understanding. Accordingly, we must abandon the quest for cumulative knowledge as in the natural sciences and search instead for insights that will expand our vision and increase our wisdom. It will be neither possible nor desirable to isolate the study of international relations from the social and normative milieus in which politics takes place.

Second, scholars should begin to think in terms of theory that unites the several subfields of political science (that unfortunate word again) and is, as well, determinedly interdisciplinary. Politics is politics, a phenomenon that is not the exclusive province of any particular discipline and that regularly crosses legal boundaries. Normative/legal boundaries are not necessarily political boundaries. Our understanding of war and peace, for example, is likely to remain stunted as long as our research of them is part of "the untidy offshoot of the study of the state." War is political violence—albeit organized violence—but can we assume it is a unique species of violence? We need not rehearse once more the logical and empirical errors that flow from assuming a dichotomy of "interstate" and "domestic" arenas, yet we should certainly keep them in mind.

Third, we must take seriously our commitment to study behavior, rather than institutions and norms, except insofar as institutions and norms actually condition behavior. The influence that the state concept exercises on our imagination inhibits our ability to discern real behavior. It encourages facile and colorful—but sterile—anthropomorphic thinking and "analyses." Rather than expecting to find and account for "state behavior," we would do better to observe and attempt to trace the source(s) of the behavior of those in defined political decisionmaking roles. Instead of organizing ourselves as comparativists, internationalists, Americanists, and so forth, we might organize some research around issues and roles.

Fourth, to the extent that we continue to look for collective behavior, we have to appreciate that human beings have loyalties to a rich and constantly changing galaxy of groups. The world has long been a crazy-quilt of polities and other groups; foci of authority with varying territorial scope, power, and legitimacy; distinct in some respects and overlapping, layered, and linked in others; competing and sometimes cooperating in a quest for the allegiance of persons and a role in the process of allocating values that are almost always in limited supply. Even though it is reasonable to suspect that there may be a relationship between political behavior and the full range of human loyalties, the national/international bifurcation discourages us from exploring all the implications.

Fifth, as the foregoing suggests, if we are going to make any genuine progress in what is coming to be a moribund field, we are going to have to become analytical adults and give up our conceptual teddy bears. We have to be prepared to jettison concepts that have had plenty of time to demonstrate their inutility. Let us regard "state," as most of us now do "nation," primarily as a normative idea that has empirical validity only in certain respects in specific cases. Concepts like "power center" have no more inherent meaning than "state," but, at a minimum, they serve an extremely useful function in forcing us to reconsider some of our comfortable delusions.

Sixth and finally, we would hope that our analyses will be firmly grounded in history and, when relevant, even prehistory. Too many "social scientists" (except historians, of course) are ahistorical, assuming that the past has little or no relevance for those of us in the present. Nothing could be further from the truth. Why study the past? One reason, perhaps the least important for our purposes, is that the past is simply there and needs to be analyzed with a "modern" eye. Historians rightly worry about the distortions that enter in—about our inability to see the past as those who lived it; but surely there is the counterargument that the people living in any given time were too close to comprehend its full significance. Another reason for looking backward is that history does repeat itself *to some extent*. Recall our earlier comments about today's world being a "living museum" of past political forms and ideas. The Greeks had "regimes"; realist thought is as old as Thucydides, Kautilya, and Machiavelli; "empires" of various descriptions persist; many ethnic identities have ancient roots; and so on and on. Finally, we urgently need to know what is unique about the present. Mann observes: "World history develops. Through historical comparison we can see that the most significant problems of our time are novel. That is why they are difficult to solve: They are interstitial to institutions that deal effectively with the more traditional problems for which they were set up."[222]

In sum, accepting our normative foundations by no means requires that we abandon systematic inquiry and generalization. We can and will continue to build theory much more successfully when we abandon "scientific" pretensions and the conceptual baggage that has only weighted us down intellectually. We need to launch a voyage of discovery into largely uncharted seas.

For us personally, this will mean undertaking historically grounded analyses of shifting patterns of authority: what these have been in specific eras, the extent to which they have or have not changed over time, and the factors accounting for persistence and change. We assume that there is a strong reciprocal relationship between the normative temper of societies and the distribution/redistribution of political loyalties. Polities have been shaped by powerful ideas—directly political or religious, social, economic, or scientific—even as authorities have encouraged some ideas and tried to suppress others. But numerous other factors have also been at work, such as major unanticipated events, the state of technology for military use and civilian production, the availability and accumulation of resources, and the appearance of "great" leaders.[223] Charting which particular factors have been most important and their impact on evolving (and devolving) authority patterns is part of our own personal voyage of discovery.

Let others set intellectual sail wherever their normative breezes blow. We do hope, however, that they will leave the shoals of "the state" far behind.

Notes

1. Yale H. Ferguson and Richard W. Mansbach, *The Elusive Quest: Theory and International Politics* (Columbia, SC: The University of South Carolina Press, 1988), chap. 5. Both authors wish to thank the Rutgers Research Council, and Professor Ferguson wishes to express his appreciation for the grant support provided by the Rutgers University Graduate School-Newark, as well as for visiting fellowships from the Centre of International Studies and Clare Hall at the University of Cambridge, during his 1986-1987 sabbatical leave. Our thanks, as well, to Michael K. O'Leary and David Wilsford for their unusually thoughtful and constructive criticisms of an earlier draft of this book.

2. David Held, "Introduction: Central Perspectives on the Modern State," in David Held, et al., *States and Societies* (Oxford, England: Martin Robertson in association with The Open University, 1983), 1.

3. It was this concern that prompted us to examine the concept of "international actor" over a decade ago. See Richard W. Mansbach, Yale H. Ferguson, and Donald E. Lampert, *The Web of World Politics: Nonstate Actors in the Global System* (Englewood Cliffs, NJ: Prentice-Hall, 1976). At that time we argued that among the factors accounting for the longevity of the concept were the relatively easy availability of aggregate data involving states, the desire of scholars to work with readily comparable data, and their preference for units of analysis that did not overlap. We have no reason to revise that assessment. Instead, we have concluded that the problem has significantly deeper sources than we originally suspected.

4. F.H. Hinsley, *Sovereignty*, 2nd ed. (Cambridge, England: Cambridge University Press, 1986), 28.

5. J.M. Wallace-Hadrill, *The Barbarian West 400–1000*, 4th ed. (Oxford, England: Basil Blackwell, 1985), 160–161.

6. Susan Reynolds, *Kingdoms and Communities in Western Europe, 900–1300* (Oxford, England: Oxford University Press, 1984).

7. J.M. Wallace-Hadrill, *The Barbarian West*, 161.

8. Susan Reynolds, *Kingdoms and Communities in Western Europe*, 330–331.

9. Ibid., 339.

10. Wallace-Hadrill rightly cautions against making too much of the theme of conflict: "No untruth is blacker than that which represents early medieval kingship and aristocracy as two fundamentally opposed forces. Tenth-century kingship was not so much weakened as circumscribed. Medieval men had no use for weakness and certainly never sought it in their kings" (161). However, to recognize that all was not conflict should not be to err in the opposite direction. How opposed is "fundamentally opposed," and how "weakened" is "circumscribed"? These are issues of more than semantic significance.

11. Perry Anderson, *Lineages of the Absolutist State* (London: New Left Books, 1974; Verso Edition, 1979), 17. See also especially: Reinhard Bendix, *Kings or People: Power and the Mandate to Rule* (Berkeley, CA: University of California Press, 1978); K. Dyson, *The State Traditions in Western Europe* (Oxford, England: Martin Robertson, 1980); V.C. Kiernan, *State and Society in Europe 1550–1650* (Oxford, England: Basil Blackwell, 1980); Gianfranco Poggi, *The Development of the Modern State* (London: Hutchinson, 1978); and Charles Tilley, ed., *The Formation of National States in Western Europe* (Princeton, NJ: Princeton University Press, 1975).

12. Roger King, *The State in Modern Society: New Directions in Political Sociology* (London: Macmillan, 1986), 39–40.

13. Michael Mann quoted in Bill Jordan, *The State: Authority and Autonomy* (Oxford, England: Basil Blackwell, 1985), 151.

14. Perry Anderson, *Lineages of the Absolutist State*, 143.

15. Bill Jordan, *The State*, 152.

16. See Perry Anderson, *Lineages of the Absolutist State*, 35–39.

17. Roger King, *The State in Modern Society*, 41.

18. Reinhard Bendix, *Kings or People*, 32.

19. Perry Anderson, *Lineages of the Absolutist State*, 24–25.

20. Ibid., 28.

21. F.H. Hinsley, *Sovereignty*, 110.

22. Ibid., 120.

23. James Anderson, "Absolutism and Other Ancestors," in James Anderson, ed., *The Rise of the Modern State* (Brighton, England: Wheatsheaf Books, 1986), 39.

24. Held, "Introduction," 15–17.

25. Bill Jordan, *The State*, 111.

26. E.H. Carr, "States and Nationalism: The Nation in European History" in Held, *States and Societies*, 185. Tom Nairn similarly observes: "Romanticism was the cultural mode of the nationalist dynamic, the cultural 'language' which alone made possible the formation of the new inter-class communities required by it. In that context, all romanticism's well-known features—the search for inwardness, the trust in feeling or instinct, the attitude to 'nature,' the cult of the particular and mistrust of the 'abstract,' etc.—make sense." "Nationalism and the Uneven Geography of Development" in Held, *States and Societies*, 200.

27. Held, "Introduction," 23–31.

28. John A. Hall, *Powers and Liberties: The Causes and Consequences of the Rise of the West* (Hammondsworth, England: Penguin, 1986), 40.

29. Adda B. Bozeman, *Politics and Culture in International History* (Princeton, NJ: Princeton University Press, 1960), 120.

30. See Hans J. Morgenthau, *Politics Among Nations: The Struggle for Power and Peace*, any edition.

31. Hans J. Morgenthau, *Politics Among Nations*, 5th ed. (New York: Knopf, 1973), 8.

32. J.P. Nettl, "The State as a Conceptual Variable," *World Politics*, 20:4 (July 1968), 559.

33. Stephen D. Krasner, "Approaches to the State: Alternative Conceptions and Historical Dynamics," *Comparative Politics*, 16:2 (January 1984), 223.

34. Stephen D. Krasner, "State Power and the Structure of International Trade," *World Politics*, 28:3 (April 1976), 317.

35. Stephen D. Krasner, "Approaches to the State," 244. By 1981, David Easton confidently declared: "The state, a concept that many of us thought had been polished off a quarter of a century ago, has now risen from the grave, to haunt us once again." "The Political System Besieged by the State," *Political Theory* (August 1981), 303. See also Gordon L. Clark and Michael Dear, *State Apparatus: Structures and Language of Legitimacy* (Boston: Allen & Unwin, 1984), 60.

36. Sabino Cassese, "The Rise and Decline of the Notion of State," *International Political Science Review* 7:2 (April 1986), 121.

37. J.W. Burton, *Systems, States, Diplomacy and Rules* (New York: Cambridge University Press, 1968), 9. Burton's imaginative conceptualization serves to counter approaches that reify the state; it also corrects the traditional overemphasis on anarchy and system decentralization as determinants of behavior. Unfortunately, it is also rather useless for empirical purposes.

38. Donald J. Puchala, *International Politics Today* (New York:

Harper & Row, 1971), 28.

39. Bertrand Badie and Pierre Birnbaum, *The Sociology of the State*, trans. Arthur Goldhammer (Chicago: University of Chicago Press, 1983), 139–140.

40. Ronald Cohen, "Introduction" in Ronald Cohen and Elman R. Service, eds., *Origins of the State: The Anthropology of Political Evolution* (Philadelphia: ISHI, 1978), 8. For intriguing support from the perspective of natural selection theory that "the state" emerged from processes of both cooperation and conflict, see Roger D. Masters, "The Biological Nature of the State," *World Politics*, 35:2 (January 1983), 161–193.

41. Ronald Cohen, "Introduction" in Ronald Cohen and Elman R. Service, eds., *Origins of the State*, 8.

42. Ibid., 2. As we suggest elsewhere in this analysis, Cohen's personal definition is essentially Weberian. See also Ronald Cohen, "State Origins: A Reappraisal" in Henri J.M. Claessen and Peter Skalnik, eds., *The Early State* (The Hague, The Netherlands: Mouton Publishers, 1978), 31–75. Two additional essays in the first volume of the GSIS series are particularly useful: the editors' "The Early State: Theories and Hypotheses," 3–29; and Anatoli M. Khazanov, "Some Theoretical Problems of the Study of the Early State," 77–92.

43. Jonathan Haas, *The Evolution of the Prehistoric State* (New York: Columbia University Press, 1982), 2–3.

44. Jonathan Haas, "Introduction" in Haas, Shelia Pozorski, and Thomas Pozorski, eds., *The Origins and Development of the Andean State* (Cambridge, England: Cambridge University Press, 1987), 2.

45. Ernest Gellner, *Nations and Nationalism* (Ithaca, NY: Cornell University Press, 1983), 5. Emphasis in original. See also: George Modelski, "Agraria and Industria: Two Models of the International System" in Klaus Knorr and Sidney Verba, eds., *The International System* (Princeton, NJ: Princeton University Press, 1961), 125ff; and Roger D. Masters, "World Politics as a Primitive Political System," *World Politics*, 16:4 (July 1964), 595–619.

46. Bertrand Badie and Pierre Birnbaum, *The Sociology of the State*, 65.

47. Ibid., 103.

48. Ibid., 60.

49. Ibid., 105.

50. Ibid., 105–115.

51. Ibid., 103–104.

52. Morton H. Fried, "The State, the Chicken, and the Egg: or What Came First?" in Ronald Cohen and Elman R. Service, eds., *Origins of the State*, 37.

53. Oran R. Young, "The Actors in World Politics," in James N. Rosenau, Vincent Davis, and Maurice A. East, eds., *The Analysis of International Politics* (New York: Free Press, 1972), 127.

54. For example, see Adda B. Bozeman, *Politics and Culture in International History*; Robert G. Wesson, *State Systems: International Pluralism, Politics, and Culture* (New York: Free Press, 1978); Allen W. Johnson and Timothy Earle, *The Evolution of Human Societies: From Foraging Group to Agrarian State* (Stanford, CA: Stanford University Press, 1987); S.N. Eisenstadt, *The Political Systems of Empires* (New York: Free Press, 1963); John H. Kautsky, *The Politics of Aristocratic Empires* (Chapel Hill, NC: University of North Carolina Press, 1982); M.I. Finley, *Politics in the Ancient World* (Cambridge, England: Cambridge University Press, 1983); John A. Armstrong, *Nations before Nationalism* (Chapel Hill, NC: University of North Carolina Press, 1982); Anthony D. Smith, *The Ethnic Origins of Nations* (Oxford, England: Basil Blackwell, 1986); and John A. Hall, ed., *States in History* (Oxford, England: Oxford University Press, 1986).

55. Charles W. Kegley, Jr. and Eugene R. Wittkopf, *World Politics: Trends and Transformation*, 2nd ed. (New York: St. Martin's Press, 1985), fn. 78–79.

56. David Vital, "Back to Machiavelli," in Klaus Knorr and James N. Rosenau, eds., *Contending Approaches to International Politics* (Princeton, NJ: Princeton University Press, 1969), 155–156. Emphasis in original.

57. Oran R. Young, "The Actors in World Politics," 131. See also Richard W. Mansbach, Yale H. Ferguson, and Donald E. Lampert, *The Web of World Politics*, 22–25.

58. William W. Bishop, Jr., *International Law: Cases and Materials*, 3rd ed. (Boston: Little, Brown, 1971), 306–307.

59. Bruce M. Russett and Harvey Starr, *World Politics: The Menu for Choice* (San Francisco: W.H. Freeman, 1981), 68. Emphasis in original.

60. Yet, it is precisely the urge to generalize that defines the modern social scientist.

61. See, for example, J. David Singer, *The Wages of War, 1816-1965: A Statistical Handbook* (New York: Wiley, 1972). Efforts by COW scholars to test hypotheses about the onset of war using such intervening variables as status ordering and alliance aggregation are complicated by uncertainty as to the comparability of the units that constituted the global system during different historical eras.

62. This is the thrust of the model advanced in F.H. Hinsley, *Sovereignty*.

63. John A. Hall, *States in History*, 16–17.

64. James N. Rosenau, "Before Cooperation: Hegemons, Regimes, and Habit-Driven Actors in World Politics," *International Organization*, 40:4 (Autumn 1986), 886.

65. Ibid., 887. Recently, Rosenau has taken the additional step of postulating a "multi-centric world" of "sovereignty-free actors" coexisting with a "state-centric system." James N. Rosenau,

"Patterned Chaos in Global Life: Structure and Process in the Two Worlds of World Politics," unpublished manuscript (Los Angeles: Institute for Transnational Studies, University of Southern California, April 1987), 21–28.

66. On city-states as a phenomenon throughout history, see also Peter Burke, "City-States" in John A. Hall, ed., *States in History*, 136–153.

67. M.I. Finley, *The Ancient Greeks* (Hammondsworth, England: Penguin, 1977), 54–55.

68. Ibid., 56.

69. Ibid., 59–60.

70. John H. Kautsky, *The Politics of Aristocratic Empires*, 344–345.

71. S.N. Eisenstadt, *The Political Systems of Empires*, 307.

72. Ibid., 338.

73. Ibid., 359–360.

74. James N. Anderson, "Absolutism and Other Ancestors," 35.

75. John H. Herz, *International Politics in the Atomic Age* (New York: Columbia University Press, 1959), chaps. 2–4. See also John H. Herz, *The Nation-State and the Crisis of World Politics* (New York: David McKay, 1976), chaps. 3 and 8.

76. Roger King, *The State in Modern Society*, 49.

77. Perry Anderson, *Lineages of the Absolutist State*, 51.

78. John H. Kautsky, *The Politics of Aristocratic Empires*, 236–237.

79. Ibid., 237.

80. John A. Hall, "Introduction," 15.

81. Michael Mann, "The Autonomous Power of the State: Its Origins, Mechanisms and Results," in John A. Hall, ed., *States in History*, 108–136.

82. John A. Hall, "Introduction," 15.

83. Penry Williams, *The Tudor Regime* (Oxford, England: Oxford University Press, paperback edition revised 1981), 463.

84. Ibid., 458.

85. Ibid., 463.

86. J.P. Nettl observes: "It is significant that the word *l'État* in French should be the only one normally beginning with a capital letter." ("The State as a Conceptual Variable," 567.)

87. Norbert Elias refers to the process as the "Courtization of Warriors." See his *State Formation and Civilization*, trans. by Edmund Jephcott (Oxford, England: Basil Blackwell, 1982), 258–270.

88. Bertrand Badie and Pierre Birnbaum, *The Sociology of the State*, 114.

89. Ibid., 105.

90. Peter Worsley, *The Three Worlds: Culture and World Development* (Chicago: University of Chicago Press, 1984), 273.

91. Robert Wesson, *State Systems*, 142.

92. James Anderson, "Absolutism and Other Ancestors," 39. Emphasis in original.

93. Ernest Gellner, *Nations and Nationalism*, 56.

94. Anthony D. Smith, *The Ethnic Origins of Nations*, chap. 1. A book that should be read in conjunction with Smith's is John A. Armstrong, *Nations Before Nationalism*. In addition, see Anthony D. Smith, "State-Making and Nation-Building" in James A. Hall, ed., *States in History*, 228–263. Among the extensive literature on nationalism, see also especially J. Breuilly, *Nationalism and the State* (Manchester, England: Manchester University Press, 1982); Hugh Seton-Watson, *Nations and States* (Boulder, CO: Westview Press, 1977); Hans Kohn, *The Idea of Nationalism*, 2nd ed. (New York: Macmillan, 1967); Louis L. Snyder, *The Meaning of Nationalism* (New Brunswick, NJ: Rutgers University Press, 1954) and *Global Mini-Nationalisms: Autonomy or Independence* (Westport, CT: Greenwood Press, 1982); *Ethnicity and Regionalism*, topical issue of *International Political Science Review* 6:2 (1985); and Frederick Hertz, *Nationality in History and Politics* (New York: Humanities Press, 1944).

95. Anthony D. Smith, *The Ethnic Origins of Nations*, 17.

96. Ernest Gellner, *Nations and Nationalism*, 34.

97. Peter Worsley, *The Three Worlds*, 292.

98. Ernest Gellner, *Nations and Nationalism*, 55–56.

99. Peter Worsley, *The Three Worlds*, 252.

100. C.H. Titus, "A Nomenclature in Political Science," *American Political Science Review* 25:1 (March 1931), 45. See also James N. Rosenau, "The State in an Era of Cascading Politics: Wavering Concept, Widening Competence, Withering Colossus, or Weathering Change?" Paper delivered to the International Political Science Association, Paris (July 1985), 9.

101. Alessandro Passerin D'Entreves, *The Notion of the State: An Introduction to Political Theory* (London: Oxford University Press, 1967), 96.

102. Clifford Geertz, *Negara: The Theatre State in Nineteenth Century Bali* (Princeton, NJ: Princeton University Press, 1981).

103. J.P. Nettl, "The State as a Conceptual Variable," 560.

104. F.H. Hinsley, *Sovereignty*, 1. Hinsley's is a brilliant study, by far the best to date, of the historical evolution of the concept.

105. Alan James, *Sovereign Statehood: The Basis of International Society* (London: Allen & Unwin, 1986), 25.

106. This postwar development is not unprecedented. The breakup of the Austro-Hungarian, Russian, and Turkish Empires as a consequence of World War I and the spreading of the "national principle" by Western liberals produced a host of weak and economically dependent states in central Europe and the Balkans that proved ready prey for Nazi influence in the 1930s. Arguably, the

erosion of the Roman Empire had similar consequences, and these were manifested in the extreme localization of authority.

107. Peter Worsley, *The Three Worlds*, 290.

108. Ibid.

109. Ibid., 289.

110. W. Raymond Duncan, *Latin American Politics: A Developmental Approach* (New York: Praeger, 1976), 121.

111. Anthony D. Smith, "State-Making and Nation-Building," 229.

112. Quoted in Bertrand Badie and Pierre Birnbaum, *The Sociology of the State*, 12.

113. Ibid., 28.

114. Ibid., 27.

115. Ibid., 56.

116. Ibid., 49.

117. Ibid., 60.

118. Ibid., 62.

119. Ibid., 100–101. See also Howard J. Wiarda, *Ethnocentrism in Foreign Policy: Can We Understand the Third World?* (Washington, DC: American Enterprise Institute for Public Policy Research, 1985). On participation, see especially Samuel P. Huntington and Joan M. Nelson, *No Easy Choice: Political Participation in Developing Countries* (Cambridge, MA: Harvard University Press, 1976).

120. For a careful analysis of Weber's writings on the state and citations to his major works, see Bertrand Badie and Pierre Birnbaum, *The Sociology of the State*, 17–24. We have drawn heavily on Badie and Birnbaum in our discussions of Weber, as well as of Emile Durkheim and Talcott Parsons *infra*. In addition, see David Held, "Introduction," 34–40, on whose work we have also drawn here and elsewhere.

121. Eric A. Nordlinger, *On the Autonomy of the Democratic State* (Cambridge, MA: Harvard University Press, 1981).

122. Bertrand Badie and Pierre Birnbaum, *The Sociology of the State*, 23–24.

123. David Held, "Introduction," 36–37.

124. Ibid., 39–40.

125. David Held, "Introduction," 34. See also Goren Therborn, "Karl Marx Returning: The Welfare State and Neo-Marxist, Corporatist and Statist Theories," *International Political Science Review* 7:2 (April 1986), 131–164.

126. Nicos Poulantzas, *State, Power, Socialism*, trans. by Patrick Camiller (London: New Left Books, 1978), 7.

127. Stephen D. Krasner, *Defending the National Interest: Raw Materials Investments and U.S. Foreign Policy* (Princeton, NJ: Princeton University Press, 1978), 21. For a succinct description of the Marxist model of international relations, see Wojciech Kostecki, "A Marxist Paradigm of International Relations," *International Studies Notes*, 12:1 (Fall 1985), 19–21.

128. David Held, "Introduction," 31–33.

129. Ralph Milibrand, *The State in Contemporary Society* (London: Weidenfeld & Nicolson, 1969).

130. Nicos Poulantzas, *State, Power, Socialism.*

131. See especially Robert A. Dahl, *A Preface to Democratic Theory* (Chicago: University of Chicago Press, 1956); and David B. Truman, *The Governmental Process* (New York: Knopf, 1951).

132. Stephen D. Krasner, *Defending the National Interest*, 27.

133. See especially Charles E. Lindblom, *Politics and Markets* (New York: Basic Books, 1977).

134. See, for example, David Collier, ed., *The New Authoritarianism in Latin America* (Princeton, NJ: Princeton University Press, 1979).

135. See, for example, Gerhard Lehmbruch and Philippe C. Schmitter, eds., *Patterns of Corporate Policy-Making* (Beverly Hills, CA: Sage, 1982); and Philippe C. Schmitter, "Democratic Theory and Neocorporatist Practice," *Social Research* 50:4 (Winter 1983), 885–928.

136. Charles W. Kegley, Jr. and Eugene R. Wittkopf, *American Foreign Policy: Pattern and Process*, 2nd ed. (New York: St. Martin's, 1982), 516–517.

137. Richard J. Barnet, *Roots of War: The Men and Institutions Behind U.S. Foreign Policy* (Baltimore, MD: Penguin, 1973), 4–5.

138. Thomas R. Dye, *Who's Running America? The Conservative Years*, 4th ed. (Englewood Cliffs, NJ: Prentice-Hall, 1986), 273–274.

139. Ibid., 267.

140. Ibid., 268. Emphasis in original.

141. Ibid., 271.

142. Ibid., 272–273.

143. Graham T. Allison, *Essence of Decision: Explaining the Cuban Missile Crisis* (Boston: Little, Brown, 1971), 164. On the governmental (bureaucratic) politics approach, see also, especially: Graham T. Allison and Morton H. Halperin, "Bureaucratic Politics: A Paradigm and Some Policy Implications," in Raymond Tanter and R.H. Ullman, eds., *Theory and Practice in International Relations* (Princeton, NJ: Princeton University Press, 1972), 40–79; Morton H. Halperin, *Bureaucratic Politics and Foreign Policy* (Washington, DC: The Brookings Institution, 1974); and Morton H. Halperin and Arnold Kantor, eds., *Readings in Foreign Policy: A Bureaucratic Perspective* (Boston: Little, Brown, 1973).

144. For such a critique, see Yale H. Ferguson and Richard W. Mansbach, *The Elusive Quest*, chap. 7.

145. Kim Richard Nossal, "Bureaucratic Politics and the Westminster Model," in Robert O. Matthews, Arthur G. Rubinoff, and Janice Gross Stein, eds., *International Conflict and Conflict Management: Readings in World Politics* (Scarborough, Ontario: Prentice-Hall of Canada, 1984), 125. See also Kenneth N. Waltz,

Foreign Policy and Domestic Politics (Boston: Little, Brown, 1967).

146. Stephen D. Krasner, "Are Bureaucracies Important? (Or Allison Wonderland)," *Foreign Policy* 7 (Summer 1972), 179.

147. Stephen D. Krasner, "Approaches to the State," 224–225.

148. Eric A. Nordlinger, *On the Autonomy of the Democratic State*, 11.

149. Ibid., 9–10.

150. Ibid., 8.

151. Ibid., 7.

152. Ibid., 186–187. Emphasis in original.

153. Devices such as cabinet responsibility in Great Britain perpetuate the same myth.

154. Manfred Wilhelmy, "Politics, Bureaucracy, and Foreign Policy in Chile" in Heraldo Muñoz and Joseph S. Tulchin, eds., *Latin American Nations in World Politics* (Boulder, CO: Westview Press, 1984), 50.

155. Alan James, *Sovereign Statehood*, especially 180ff.

156. Ibid., 276–277.

157. See especially Robert H. Jackson and Carl G. Rosberg, "Why Africa's Weak States Persist: The Empirical and the Juridical in Statehood," *World Politics*, 35:1 (October 1982), 1–24; Robert H. Jackson, "Negative Sovereignty in Sub-Saharan Africa," *Review of International Studies*, 12:4 (October 1986), 246–264; and Robert H. Jackson, "African States and International Theory," paper delivered at the British International Studies Association annual meeting, University of Reading, Reading, England, 16 December 1986.

158. Robert H. Jackson, "African States and International Theory," 29.

159. Ibid., 4–7. See also James Mayall, "The Variety of States," paper delivered at the British International Studies Association annual meeting, University of Reading, Reading, England, 16 December 1986.

160. Robert H. Jackson, "African States and International Theory," 33.

161. Ibid., 36–38. The reference is to J.D.B. Miller, "Sovereignty as a Source of Vitality for the State," *Review of International Studies*, 12:2 (April 1986), 79–91.

162. Robert H. Jackson and Carl G. Rosberg, "Why Africa's Weak States Persist," 13–14.

163. John Gerard Ruggie, "Continuity and Transformation in the World Polity: Toward a Neorealist Synthesis," *World Politics*, 35:2 (January 1983), 275–276.

164. Ibid., footnote 39, 276. The present authors see no reason to alter those views.

165. Kenneth N. Waltz, *Theory of International Politics* (Reading, MA: Addison-Wesley, 1979), 96. Hinsley argues along the same lines that one should not "associate the attribute of sovereignty with the

possession by the state of freedom to act as it chooses instead of with the absence over and above the state of a superior authority. To do that is to confuse the situation to which states may often have aspired, but have never in fact enjoyed, with the opposite condition from which the concept of sovereignty in its international version historically obtained its relevance and from which it continues to derive it—that condition in which a collection of states, all insisting on their independence, were brought to recognize that they do not exist in isolation but are forced to live with other states." (*Sovereignty*, 226.)

166. John Gerard Ruggie, "Continuity and Transformation in the World Polity," footnote 39, 276.

167. Ibid., 276. Emphasis in original.

168. Ibid., 280. Emphasis in original.

169. See, for example, Robert O. Keohane, ed., *Neorealism and Its Critics* (New York: Columbia University Press, 1986).

170. F.H. Hinsley, *Sovereignty*, 225.

171. Alan James, *Sovereign Statehood*, 148.

172. See also Yale H. Ferguson and Richard W. Mansbach, *The Elusive Quest*, chap. 8.

173. Kenneth N. Waltz, *Theory of International Politics*, 98–99.

174. See especially Immanuel Wallerstein, *The Capitalist World-Economy* (Cambridge, England: Cambridge University Press, 1979), *The Politics of the World Economy: The States, the Movements, and Civilization* (Cambridge, England: Cambridge University Press, 1984), and *The Modern World-System: Capitalist Agriculture and the Origins of the European World-Economy in the Sixteenth Century* (New York: Academic Press, 1974). Useful critiques of Wallerstein include: Aristide R. Zolberg, "Origins of the Modern World System: A Missing Link," *World Politics*, 33:2 (January 1981), 253–281; Robert Brenner, "The Origins of Capitalist Development: A Critique of Neo-Smithian Marxism," *New Left Review* 104 (July/August 1976), 25–92; Theda Skocpol, "Wallerstein's World Capitalist System: A Theoretical Critique," *American Journal of Sociology* 82:5 (March 1977), 1075–1090; and Peter Worsley, "One World or Three? A Critique of the World System Theory of Immanuel Wallerstein," reprinted in David Held, ed., *States and Societies*, 504–525.

175. Kenneth N. Waltz, *Theory of International Politics*, 195.

176. Immanuel Wallerstein, *The Modern World System*, 357.

177. Stephen D. Krasner, "Structural Causes and Regime Consequences: Regimes as Intervening Variables," in Stephen D. Krasner, ed., "International Regimes," special issue of *International Organization* 36:2 (Spring 1982), 185–186.

178. Robert O. Keohane, *After Hegemony: Cooperation and Discord in the World Economy* (Princeton, NJ: Princeton University Press, 1984), 64.

179. Donald J. Puchala and Raymond F. Hopkins, "International

Regimes: Lessons from Inductive Analysis," in Krasner, ed., "International Regimes," 247. Emphasis in original. In the same issue see also Oran R. Young, "Regime Dynamics: The Rise and Fall of International Regimes," 277–297.

180. Susan Strange, "*Cave! Hic Dragones*: A Critique of Regime Analysis," in Krasner, ed., "International Regimes," 487.

181. Two representative works from this era are Robert O. Keohane and Joseph S. Nye, Jr., eds., *Transnational Relations and World Politics* (Cambridge, MA: Harvard University Press, 1972); and Robert O. Keohane and Joseph S. Nye, Jr., *Power and Interdependence: World Politics in Transition* (Boston: Little, Brown, 1977).

182. See, for example, Peter J. Katzenstein, "International Interdependence: Some Long-Range Trends and Recent Changes," *International Organization* 29:4 (Autumn 1975), 1021–1034.

183. Richard N. Rosecrance, A. Alexandroff, W. Koehler, S. Laqueur, and J. Stocker, "Whither Interdependence?" *International Organization* 31:3 (Summer 1977), 426.

184. Ibid., 426–427. Emphasis in original.

185. Robert O. Keohane and Joseph S. Nye, Jr., *Power and Interdependence: World Politics in Transition*, 9–10.

186. Ibid., 11–19.

187. Kenneth N. Waltz, "Will the Future Be Like the Past?" in Nissan Oren, ed., *When Patterns Change: Turning Points in International Politics* (New York: St. Martin's Press, 1984), 26. Waltz's definition of interdependence is very similar to that of Keohane and Nye.

188. Richard N. Rosecrance, et al., "Whither Interdependence?" 441–444. Differing conceptualizations of interdependence naturally lead to measurement disputes. See, for example, Mary Ann Tetreault, "Measuring Interdependence," *International Organization* 34:3 (Summer 1980), 429–443; Richard N. Rosecrance and William Gutowitz, "Measuring Interdependence: A Response," *International Organization* 35:3 (Summer 1981), 553–556, 557–560.

189. Stephen D. Cohen, *The Making of United States International Economic Policy*, 2nd ed. (New York: Praeger, 1981), 85, 89.

190. Robert O. Keohane, *After Hegemony*, 5.

191. Kenneth N. Waltz, "Will the Future Be Like the Past?" 27.

192. See James A. Caporaso, ed., "Dependence and Dependency in the Global System," special issue, *International Organization* 32:1 (Winter 1978).

193. This is perhaps not surprising in view of the potent ideological commitments evident in earlier discussions of this issue. See, for example, Osvaldo Sunkel, "The Crisis of the Nation-State in Latin America: Challenge and Response," in Yale H. Ferguson and

Walter F. Weiker, eds., *Continuing Issues in International Politics* (Pacific Palisades, CA: Goodyear, 1973); Sunkel, "Big Business and 'Dependencia': A Latin American View," *Foreign Affairs* 50:3 (April 1972), 517–531; Fernando Enrique Cardoso, *Dependencia y desarrollo en América Latina* (Mexico: Siglo Veintiuno Editores, 1969); and Theontonio dos Santos, *El Nuevo carácter de la dependencia* (Santiago, Chile: Cuadernos de CESO, 1968).

194.   Alberto van Klaveren, "The Analysis of Latin American Foreign Policies: Theoretical Perspectives," in Heraldo Muñoz and Joseph S. Tulchin, eds., *Latin American Nations in World Politics*, 8.

195.   William E. Brock, "Trade and Debt: The Vital Linkage," *Foreign Affairs* 62:5 (Summer 1984), 1045.

196.   Dennis K. Gordon, "Argentina's Foreign Policies in the Post-Malvinas Era," in Jennie K. Lincoln and Elizabeth G. Ferris, eds., *The Dynamics of Latin American Foreign Policies: Challenges for the 1980s* (Boulder, CO: Westview Press, 1984), 98.

197.   David Leyton-Brown, "The Nation-State and Multinational Enterprise: Erosion or Assertion," in Robert O. Matthews, Arthur G. Rubinoff, and Janice Gross Stein, eds., *International Conflict and Conflict Management*, 339. The interaction among foreign firms, governments, and bureaucracies involved in coordinating negotiations with potential investors is described in Dennis J. Encarnation and Louis T. Wells, Jr., "Sovereignty En Garde: Negotiating with Foreign Investors," *International Organization* 39:1 (Winter 1985), 47–78. See also Joseph M. Grieco, "Between Dependency and Autonomy: India's Experience with the International Computer Industry," *International Organization* 36:3 (Summer 1982), 609–632.

198.   For a counterargument to the "decline in hegemony" thesis, see Bruce M. Russett, "The Mysterious Case of Vanishing Hegemony; or, Is Mark Twain Really Dead?" *International Organization* 39:2 (Spring 1985), 207–231.

199.   Roy Licklider, *Political Power and the Arab Oil Weapon: The Experience of Five Industrial Nations* (Berkeley: University of California Press, 1988), 280, 281.

200.   On the other side, Arab leaders have for many years been constrained from taking steps toward reconciliation with Israel by fears of assassination, coup, or massive unrest. The fate of leaders such as King Abdullah of Jordan and Anwar Sadat of Egypt is sobering indeed to those who might wish to reach an agreement.

201.   A.W. DePorte, *Europe Between the Superpowers* (New Haven, CT: Yale University Press, 1979), vii.

202.   Stephen Szabo, et al., *The Successor Generation: International Perspectives* (London: Butterworth, 1983).

203.   Regime theorists correctly point out that national bureaucracies occasionally form transnational alliances in support of particular arrangements of mutual benefit. To this extent, they may

represent the other side of the coin. See, for example, Raymond F. Hopkins, "The International Role of 'Domestic' Bureaucracy," *International Organization* 30:3 (Summer 1976), 405–432. Nor are the developing countries entirely untroubled by bureaucratic "subversion," as Dennis J. Encarnation and Louis T. Wells, Jr. conclude in their survey of negotiations with foreign investors ("Sovereignty En Garde," 75): "In a few of the cases we saw, we suspect that the goals of the negotiating body were more in line with increasing benefits to the organization than with maximizing the contribution of the project to the country as a whole."

204. Roy Licklider, *Political Power and the Arab Oil Weapon*, 295.

205. James N. Rosenau, ed., *Linkage Politics* (New York: Free Press, 1969).

206. James N. Rosenau, "Pre-Theories and Theories of Foreign Policy" in R. Barry Farrell, ed., *Approaches to Comparative and International Politics* (Evanston, IL: Northwestern University Press, 1966), 27–92.

207. James N. Rosenau, "Foreign Policy as an Issue-Area" in Rosenau, ed., *Domestic Sources of Foreign Policy* (New York: Free Press, 1967), 11–50.

208. His latest statement is "The State in an Era of Cascading Politics."

209. Mansbach, Ferguson, Lampert, *The Web of World Politics*, chap. 7.

210. See Theda Skocpol, *States and Revolutions: A Comparative Analysis of France, Russia and China* (Cambridge, England; Cambridge University Press, 1979); "States and Revolutions: France, Russia and China," in David Held, ed., *States and Societies*, 151–169; and "Bringing the State Back In: Current Research," in Peter B. Evans, Dietrich Rueschemeyer, and Theda Skocpol, eds., *Bringing the State Back In* (Cambridge, England: Cambridge University Press, 1985), 3–37.

211. Theda Skocpol, *States and Revolutions*, 29.

212. Ibid., 32.

213. David Held, "Introduction," 43.

214. Ibid.

215. Skocpol, "Bringing the State Back In," 15.

216. Peter B. Evans, Dietrich Rueschemeyer, and Theda Skocpol, "On the Road Towards a More Adequate Understanding of the State," in Evans, Rueschemeyer, and Skocpol, eds., *Bringing the State Back In*, 350.

217. Michael Mann, *The Sources of Social Power: A History of Power from the Beginning to A.D. 1760* (Cambridge, England: Cambridge University Press, 1986), 37.

218. Ibid., 1–28 passim.

219. Ibid., 4.

220. Ibid., 27.

221. Dina A. Zinnes, "Prerequisites for the Study of System Transformation," in Ole R. Holsti, Randolph W. Siverson, and Alexander L. George, eds., *Change in the International System* (Boulder, CO: Westview Press, 1980), 5.

222. Mann, *The Sources of Social Power*, 32.

223. See, for example, William H. McNeill, *The Pursuit of Power: Technology, Armed Force, and Society since A.D. 1000* (Chicago: University of Chicago Press, 1982), p. 23.

Bibliography

Allison, Graham T. (1971). *Essence of Decision: Explaining the Cuban Missile Crisis* (Boston: Little, Brown).

Allison, Graham T. and Morton H. Halperin (1972). "Bureaucratic politics: A paradigm and some policy implications." In Raymond Tanter and R. H. Ullman (eds.), *Theory and Practice in International Relations* (Princeton, NJ: Princeton University Press), pp. 40-79.

Anderson, James (1986). "Absolutism and other ancestors." In James Anderson (ed.), *The Rise of the Modern State* (Brighton, England: Wheatsheaf Books), pp. 21-40.

Anderson, James (ed.) (1986). *The Rise of the Modern State* (Brighton, England: Wheatsheaf Books).

Anderson, Perry (1974). *Lineages of the Absolutist State* (London: New Left Books).

Armstrong, John A. (1982). *Nations Before Nationalism* (Chapel Hill, NC: University of North Carolina Press).

Badie, Bertrand and Pierre Birnbaum (1983). *The Sociology of the State*, trans. Arthur Goldhammer (Chicago: University of Chicago Press).

Barnet, Richard J. (1973). *Roots of War: The Men and Institutions Behind U.S. Foreign Policy* (Baltimore, MD: Penguin).

Bendix, Reinhard (1978). *Kings or People: Power and the Mandate to Rule* (Berkeley, CA: University of California Press).

Bishop, William W., Jr. (1971). *International Law: Cases and Materials*, 3rd ed. (Boston: Little, Brown).

Bozeman, Adda B. (1960). *Politics and Culture in International*

History (Princeton, NJ: Princeton University Press).

Brenner, Robert (1976). "The origins of capitalist development: A missing critique of neo-Smithian marxism." *New Left Review*, no. 104, (July/August), pp. 25-92.

Breuilly, J. (1982). *Nationalism and the State* (Manchester, England: Manchester University Press).

Brock, William E. (1984). "Trade and debt: The vital linkage. *Foreign Affairs*, vol. 62, no. 5 (Summer), pp. 1037-1057.

Burke, Peter (1986). "City-states." In John A. Hall (ed.), *States in History* (Oxford, England: Oxford University Press), pp. 137-153.

Burton, J. W. (1968). *Systems, States, Diplomacy and Rules* (New York: Cambridge University Press).

Caporaso, James A. (ed) (1978). "Dependence and dependency in the global system." Special issue, *International Organization*, vol. 32, no. 1 (Winter).

Cardoso, Fernando Enrique (1969). *Dependencia y desarrollo en América Latina* (Mexico: Siglo Veintiuno Editores).

Carr, E. H. (1983). "States and nationalism: The nation in European History." In David Held (ed.), *States and Societies* (Oxford, England: Martin Robertson in association with The Open University), pp. 181-194.

Cassese, Sabino (1986). "The rise and decline of the notion of State." *International Political Science Review*, vol. 7, no. 2 (April), pp. 120-130.

Claessen, Henri J. M. and Peter Skalnik (1978). "The early state: theories and hypotheses." In Claessen and Skalnik (eds.), *The Early State* (The Hague, The Netherlands: Mouton Publishers), pp. 77-92.

Claessen, Henri J. M. and Peter Skalnik (eds.) (1978). *The Early State* (The Hague, The Netherlands: Mouton Publishers).

Clark, Gordon L. and Michael Dear (1984). *State Apparatus: Structures and Languages of Legitimacy* (Boston: Allen & Unwin).

Cohen, Ronald (1978). "Introduction." In Cohen and Elman R. Service (eds.), *Origins of the State: The Anthropology of Political Evolution* (Philadelphia: ISHI).

Cohen, Ronald (1978). "State origins: A reappraisal." In Henri J. M. Claessen and Peter Skalnik (eds.), *The Early State* (The Hague, The Netherlands: Mouton Publishers), pp. 31-75.

Cohen, Ronald and Elman R. Service (eds.) (1978). *Origins of the State: The Anthropology of Political Evolution* (Philadelphia: ISHI).

Cohen, Stephen D. (1981). *The Making of United States International Economic Policy*, 2nd ed. (New York: Praeger).

Collier, David (ed.) (1979). *The New Authoritarianism in Latin America* (Princeton, NJ: Princeton University Press).

Dahl, Robert A. (1956). *A Preface to Democratic Theory* (Chicago: University of Chicago Press).

DePorte, A. W. (1979). *Europe Between the Superpowers* (New Haven,

CT: Yale University Press).

Dos Santos, Theontonio (1968). *El nuevo carácter de la dependencia* (Santiago, Chile: Cuadernos de CESO).

Duncan, W. Raymond (1976). *Latin American Politics: A Developmental Approach* (New York: Praeger).

Dye, Thomas R. (1986). *Who's Running America? The Conservative Years*, 4th ed. (Englewood Cliffs, NJ: Prentice-Hall).

Dyson, K. (1980). *The State Traditions in Western Europe* (Oxford, England: Martin Robertson).

Easton, David (1981). "The political system besieged by the state." *Political Theory*, vol. 9, no. 3 (August), pp. 303-325.

Eisenstadt, S. N. (1963). *The Political Systems of Empires* (New York: Free Press).

Elias, Norbert (1982). *State Formation and Civilization*, trans. Edmund Jephcott (Oxford, England: Basil Blackwell).

Encarnation, Dennis J. and Louis T. Wells, Jr. (1985). "Sovereignty en garde: negotiating with foreign investors." *International Organization*, vol. 39, no. 1 (Winter), pp. 47-78.

Evans, Peter B., Dietrich Rueschemeyer, and Theda Skocpol (1985). "On the road towards a more adequate understanding of the state." In Evans, Rueschemeyer, and Skocpol (eds.), *Bringing the State Back In* (Cambridge, England: Cambridge University Press), pp. 347-366.

Evans, Peter B., Dietrich Rueschemeyer, and Theda Skocpol (eds.) (1985). *Bringing the State Back In* (Cambridge, England: Cambridge University Press).

Farrell, R. Barry (ed.) (1966). *Approaches to Comparative and International Politics* (Evanston, IL: Northwestern University Press).

Ferguson, Yale H. and Walter F. Weiker (eds.) (1973). *Continuing Issues in International Politics* (Pacific Palisades, CA: Goodyear).

Ferguson, Yale H. and Richard W. Mansbach (1988). *The Elusive Quest: Theory and International Politics* (Columbia, SC: University of South Carolina Press).

Finley, M. I. (1977). *The Ancient Greeks* (Hammondsworth, England: Penguin).

Finley, M. I. (1983). *Politics in the Ancient World* (Cambridge, England: Cambridge University Press).

Fried, Morton H. (1978). "The state, the chicken, and the egg: Or what came first?" In Ronald Cohen and Elman R. Service (eds.), *Origins of the State: The Anthropology of Political Evolution* (Philadelphia: ISHI), pp. 35-47.

Geertz, Clifford (1981). *Negara: The Theatre State in Nineteenth Century Bali* (Princeton, NJ: Princeton University Press).

Gellner, Ernest (1983). *Nations and Nationalism* (Ithaca, NY: Cornell University Press).

Gordon, Dennis K. (1984). "Argentina's foreign policy in the post-Malvinas era." In Jennie K. Lincoln and Elizabeth G. Ferris (eds.), *The Dynamics of Latin American Foreign Policies: Challenges for the 1980s* (Boulder, CO: Westview Press).

Grieco, Joseph M. (1982). "Between dependency and autonomy: India's experience with the international computer industry." *International Organization,* vol. 36, no. 3 (Summer), pp. 609-632.

Haas, Jonathan (1982). *The Evolution of the Prehistoric State* (New York: Columbia University Press).

Haas, Jonathan (1987). "Introduction." In Haas, Shelia Pozorski, and Thomas Pozorski (eds.), *The Origins and Development of the Andean State* (Cambridge, England: Cambridge University Press), pp. 1-4.

Haas, Jonathan, Shelia Pozorski, and Thomas Pozorski (eds.) (1987). *The Origins and Development of the Andean State* (Cambridge, England: Cambridge University Press).

Hall, John A. (1986). "Introduction." In Hall (ed.), *States in History* (Oxford, England: Oxford University Press), pp. 1-21.

Hall, John A. (ed.) (1986). *States in History* (Oxford, England: Oxford University Press).

Hall, John A. (1986). *Powers and Liberties: The Causes and Consequences of the Rise of the West* (Hammondsworth, England: Penguin).

Halperin, Morton H. (1974). *Bureaucratic Politics and Foreign Policy* (Washington, DC: Brookings Institution).

Halperin, Morton H. and Arnold Kantor (eds.) (1973). *Readings in Foreign Policy: A Bureaucratic Perspective* (Boston: Little, Brown).

Held, David (1983). "Introduction: Central perspectives on the modern state." In David Held (ed.), *States and Societies* (Oxford, England: Martin Robertson in association with The Open University), pp. 1-55.

Held, David (ed.) (1983). *States and Societies* (Oxford, England: Martin Robertson in association with The Open University).

Hertz, Frederick (1944). *Nationality in History and Politics* (New York: Humanities Press).

Herz, John H. (1959). *International Politics in the Atomic Age* (New York: Columbia University Press).

Herz, John H. (1976). *The Nation-State and the Crisis of World Politics* (New York: David McKay).

Hinsley, F. H. (1986). *Sovereignty,* 2nd ed. (Cambridge, England: Cambridge University Press).

Holsti, Ole R., Randolph W. Siverson, and Alexander L. George (eds.) (1980). *Change in the International System* (Boulder, CO: Westview Press).

Hopkins, Raymond F. (1976). "The international role of 'domestic' bureaucracy." *International Organization,* vol. 30, no. 3 (Summer), pp. 405-432.

IPSR Editorial Committee (1985). *Ethnicity and Regionalism*, issue of *International Political Science Review*, vol. 6, no. 2.

Jackson, Robert H. (1986). "African states and international theory." Paper delivered at the British International Studies Association annual meeting, University of Reading, Reading, England.

Jackson, Robert H. (1986). "Negative sovereignty in sub-saharan Africa." *Review of International Studies*, vol. 12, no. 4 (October).

Jackson, Robert H. and Carl G. Rosberg (1982). "Why Africa's weak states persist: The empirical and the juridical in statehood." *World Politics*, vol. 35, no. 1 (October), pp. 1-24.

James, Alan (1986). *Sovereign Statehood: The Basis of International Society* (London: Allen & Unwin).

Johnson, Allen W. and Timothy Earle (1987). *The Evolution of Human Societies: From Foraging Group to Early State* (Stanford, CA: Stanford University Press).

Jordan, Bill (1985). *The State: Authority and Autonomy* (Oxford, England: Basil Blackwell).

Katzenstein, Peter J. (1975). "International interdependence: Some long-range trends and recent changes." *International Organization*, vol. 29, no. 4 (Autumn), pp. 1021-1034.

Kautsky, John H. (1982). *The Politics of Aristocratic Empires* (Chapel Hill, NC: University of North Carolina Press).

Kegley, Charles W., Jr. and Eugene R. Wittkopf (1982). *American Foreign Policy: Pattern and Process*, 2nd ed. (New York: St. Martin's).

Kegley, Charles W., Jr. and Eugene R. Wittkopf (1985). *World Politics: Trends and Transformation*, 2nd ed. (New York: St. Martin's Press).

Keohane, Robert O. (1984) *After Hegemony: Cooperation and Discord in the World Economy* (Princeton, NJ: Princeton University Press).

Keohane, Robert O. (ed.) (1986). *Neorealism and Its Critics* (New York: Columbia University Press).

Keohane, Robert O. and Joseph S. Nye, Jr. (eds.) (1972). *Transnational Relations and World Politics* (Cambridge, MA: Harvard University Press).

Keohane, Robert O. and Joseph S. Nye, Jr. (1977). *Power and Interdependence: World Politics in Transition* (Boston: Little, Brown).

Khazanov, Anatoli M. (1978). "Some theoretical problems of the study of the early state." In Henri J. M. Claessen and Peter Skalnik (eds.), *The Early State* (The Hague, The Netherlands: Mouton Publishers), pp. 77-92.

Kiernan, V. C. (1980). *State and Society in Europe 1550-1650* (Oxford, England: Basil Blackwell).

King, Roger (1986). *The State in Modern Society: New Directions in Political Sociology* (London: Macmillan).

Knorr, Klaus and Sidney Verba (eds.) (1961). *The International System* (Princeton, NJ: Princeton University Press).

Knorr, Klaus and James N. Rosenau (eds.) (1969) *Contending Approaches to International Politics* (Princeton, NJ: Princeton University Press).

Kohn, Hans (1967). *The Idea of Nationalism*, 2nd ed. (New York: Macmillan).

Kostecki, Wojciech (1985). "A marxist paradigm of international relations." *International Studies Notes*, vol. 12, no. 1 (Fall).

Krasner, Stephen D. (1972). "Are bureaucracies important? (Or Allison wonderland). *Foreign Policy*, no. 7 (Summer), pp. 159-179.

Krasner, Stephen D. (1976). "State power and the structure of international trade." *World Politics*, vol. 28, no. 3 (April), pp. 317-347.

Krasner, Stephen D. (1978). *Defending the National Interest: Raw Materials Investments and U.S. Foreign Policy* (Princeton, NJ: Princeton University Press).

Krasner, Stephen D. (1982). "Structural causes and regime consequences: Regimes as intervening variables." *International Organization*, vol. 36, no. 2 (Spring), pp. 185-205.

Krasner, Stephen D. (1984). "Approaches to the state: Alternative conceptions and historical dynamics." *Comparative Politics*, vol. 16, no. 2 (January), pp. 223-246.

Lehmbruch, Gerhard and Philippe C. Schmitter (eds.) (1982). *Patterns of Corporate Policy-Making* (Beverly Hills, CA: Sage).

Leyton-Brown, David (1984). "The nation-state and multinational enterprise: Erosion or assertion." In Robert O. Matthews, Arthur G. Rubinoff, and Janice Gross Stein (eds.), *International Conflict and Conflict Management: Readings in World Politics* (Scarborough, Ontario: Prentice-Hall of Canada), pp. 330-340.

Licklider, Roy (1988). *Political Power and the Arab Oil Weapon: The Experience of Five Industrial Nations* (Berkeley, CA: University of California Press).

Lincoln, Jennie K. and Elizabeth G. Ferris (eds.) (1984). *The Dynamics of Latin American Foreign Policies: Challenges for the 1980s* (Boulder, CO: Westview Press).

Lindblom, Charles E. (1977). *Politics and Markets* (New York: Basic Books).

Mann, Michael (1986). "The autonomous power of the state: Its origins, mechanisms and results." In John A. Hall (ed.), *States in History* (Oxford, England: Oxford University Press), pp. 109-136.

Mann, Michael (1986). *The Sources of Social Power: A History of Power from the Beginning to A.D. 1760* (Cambridge, England: Cambridge University Press).

Mansbach, Richard W., Yale H. Ferguson, and Donald E. Lampert (1976). *The Web of World Politics: Nonstate Actors in the Global*

System (Englewood Cliffs, NJ: Prentice-Hall).

Masters, Roger D. (1964). "World politics as a primitive political system." *World Politics*, vol. 16, no. 4 (July), pp. 595-619.

Masters, Roger D. (1983). "The Biological Nature of the State." *World Politics*, vol. 35, no. 2 (January), pp. 161-193.

Matthews, Robert O., Arthur G. Rubinoff, and Janice Gross Stein (eds.) (1984). *International Conflict and Conflict Management: Readings in World Politics* (Scarborough, Ontario: Prentice-Hall of Canada).

Mayall, James (1986). "The variety of states." Paper delivered at the British International Studies Association annual meeting, University of Reading, Reading, England.

McNeill, William H. (1982). *The Pursuit of Power: Technology, Armed Force, and Society Since A.D. 1000* (Chicago: University of Chicago Press).

Milibrand, Ralph (1969). *The State in Contemporary Society* (London: Weidenfeld & Nicolson).

Miller, J. D. B. (1986). "Sovereignty as a source of vitality for the state." *Review of International Studies*, vol. 12, no. 2 (April), pp. 79-91.

Modelski, George (1961). "Agraria and industria: Two models of the international system." In Klaus Knorr and Sidney Verba (eds.), *The International System* (Princeton, NJ: Princeton University Press), pp. 118-143.

Morgenthau, Hans J. (1973). *Politics Among Nations: The Struggle for Power and Peace*, 5th ed. (New York: Knopf).

Muñoz, Heraldo and Joseph S. Tulchin (eds.) (1984). *Latin American Nations in World Politics* (Boulder, CO: Westview Press).

Nairn, Tom (1983). "Nationalism and the uneven geography of development." In David Held (ed.), *States and Societies* (Oxford, England: Martin Robertson in association with The Open University), pp. 195-205.

Nelson, Joan M. (1976). *No Easy Choice: Political Participation in Developing Countries* (Cambridge, MA: Harvard University Press).

Nettl, J. P. (1968). "The state as a conceptual variable." *World Politics*, vol. 20, no. 4 (July), pp. 559-592.

Nordlinger, Eric A. (1981). *On the Autonomy of the Democratic State* (Cambridge, MA: Harvard University Press).

Nossal, Kim Richard (1984). "Bureaucratic politics and the Westminster model." In Robert O. Matthews, Arthur G. Rubinoff, and Janice Gross Stein (eds.), *International Conflict and Conflict Management: Readings in World Politics* (Scarborough, Ontario: Prentice-Hall of Canada), pp. 120-127.

Oren, Nissan (ed.) (1984). *When Patterns Change: Turning Points in International Politics* (New York: St. Martin's Press).

Passerin D'Entreves, Alessandro (1967). *The Notion of the State: An Introduction to Political Theory* (London: Oxford University Press).

Poggi, Gianfranco (1978). *The Development of the Modern State* (London: Hutchinson).

Poulantzas, Nicos (1978). *State, Power, Socialism*, trans. Patrick Camiller (London: New Left Books).

Puchala, Donald J. (1971). *International Politics Today* (New York: Harper & Row).

Puchala, Donald J. and Raymond F. Hopkins (1982). "International regimes: lessons from inductive analysis." *International Organization*, vol. 36, no. 2 (Spring), pp. 245-275.

Reynolds, Susan (1984). *Kingdoms and Communities in Western Europe, 900-1300* (Oxford, England: Oxford University Press).

Rosecrance, Richard N., A. Alexandroff, W. Koehler, S. Laqueur, and J. Stocker (1977). "Whither interdependence?" *International Organization*, vol. 31, no. 3 (Summer), pp. 425-444.

Rosecrance, Richard N. and William Gutowitz (1981). "Measuring interdependence: A response." *International Organization*, vol. 35, no. 3 (Summer), pp. 553-556.

Rosenau, James N. (1966). "Pre-theories and theories of foreign policy." In R. Barry Farrell (ed.), *Approaches to Comparative and International Politics* (Evanston, IL: Northwestern University Press), pp. 27-93.

Rosenau, James N. (1967). "Foreign policy as an issue-area." In Rosenau (ed.), *Domestic Sources of Foreign Policy* (New York: Free Press), pp. 11-50.

Rosenau, James N. (1967). *Domestic Sources of Foreign Policy* (New York: Free Press).

Rosenau, James N. (ed.) (1969). *Linkage Politics* (New York: Free Press).

Rosenau, James N. (1985). "The state in an era of cascading politics: Wavering concept, withering colossus, or weathering change?" Paper delivered to the International Political Science Association, Paris (July).

Rosenau, James N. (1986). "Before cooperation: Hegemons, regimes, and habit-driven actors in world politics." *International Organization*, vol. 40, no. 4 (Autumn), pp. 849-894.

Rosenau, James N. (1987). "Patterned chaos in global life: Structure and process in the two worlds of world politics." Unpublished manuscript (Los Angeles: Institute for Transnational Studies, University of Southern California).

Rosenau, James N., Vincent Davis, and Maurice A. East (eds.) (1972). *The Analysis of International Politics* (New York: Free Press).

Ruggie, John Gerard (1983). "Continuity and transformation in the world polity: Toward a neorealist synthesis." *World Politics*, vol. 35, no. 2 (January), pp. 261-285.

Russett, Bruce M. (1985). "The mysterious case of vanishing hegemony: Or, is Mark Twain really dead?" *International Organization*, vol. 39, no. 2 (Spring), pp. 207-231.

Russett, Bruce M. and Harvey Starr (1981). *World Politics: The Menu for Choice* (San Francisco, CA: W.H. Freeman).

Schmitter, Philippe C. (1983). "Democratic theory and neocorporatist practice." *Social Research*, vol. 50, no. 4 (Winter), pp. 885-928.

Seton-Watson, Hugh (1977). *Nations and States* (Boulder, CO: Westview Press).

Singer, J. David (1972). *The Wages of War, 1816-1965: A Statistical Handbook* (New York: Wiley).

Skocpol, Theda (1977). "Wallerstein's world capitalist system: A theoretical critique." *American Journal of Sociology*, vol. 82, no. 5 (March), pp. 1075-1090.

Skocpol, Theda (1979). *States and Revolutions: A Comparative Analysis of France, Russia and China* (Cambridge, England: Cambridge University Press).

Skocpol, Theda (1983). "States and revolutions: France, Russia and China." In David Held (ed.) *States and Societies* (Oxford, England: Martin Robertson in association with The Open University), pp. 151-169.

Skocpol, Theda (1985). "Bringing the state back in: Current research." In Peter B. Evans, Dietrich Rueschemeyer, and Theda Skocpol (eds.), *Bringing the State Back In* (Cambridge, England: Cambridge University Press), pp. 3-37.

Smith, Anthony D. (1986). *The Ethnic Origins of Nations* (Oxford, England: Basil Blackwell).

Smith, Anthony D. (1986). "State-making and nation-building." In James A. Hall (ed.), *States in History* (Oxford, England: Oxford University Press), pp. 228-263.

Snyder, Louis L. (1954). *The Meaning of Nationalism* (New Brunswick, NJ: Rutgers University Press).

Snyder, Louis L. (1982). *Global Mini-Nationalisms: Autonomy or Independence?* (Westport, CT: Greenwood Press).

Strange, Susan (1982). "*Cave! Hic dragones:* A critique of regime analysis." *International Organization*, vol. 36, no. 2 (Spring), pp. 479-496.

Sunkel, Osvaldo (1972). "Big business and 'dependencia': A Latin American view." *Foreign Affairs*, vol. 50, no. 3 (April), pp. 517-531.

Sunkel, Osvaldo (1973). "The crisis of the nation-state in Latin America: Challenge and response." In Yale H. Ferguson and Walter F. Weiker (eds.), *Continuing Issues in International Politics* (Pacific Palisades, CA: Goodyear), pp. 352-368.

Szabo, Stephen, et al. (1983). *The Successor Generation: International Perspectives* (London: Butterworth).

Tanter, Raymond and R. H. Ullman (eds.) (1972). *Theory and Practice in International Relations* (Princeton, NJ: Princeton University Press).

Tetreault, Mary Ann (1980). "Measuring interdependence." *International Organization*, vol. 34, no. 3 (Summer), pp. 557-560.

Therborn, Goren (1986). "Karl Marx returning: The welfare state and neo-marxist, corporatist and statist theories." *International Political Science Review*, vol. 7, no. 2 (April), pp. 131-164.

Tilley, Charles (ed.) (1975). *The Formation of National States in Western Europe* (Princeton, NJ: Princeton University Press).

Titus, C. H. (1931). "A nomenclature in political science." *American Political Science Review*, vol. 25, no. 1 (March), pp. 45-60.

Truman, David B. (1951). *The Governmental Process* (New York: Knopf).

Van Klaveren, Alberto (1984). "The analysis of Latin American foreign policies: Theoretical perspectives." In Heraldo Muñoz and Joseph S. Tulchin (eds.), *Latin American Nations in World Politics* (Boulder, CO: Westview Press), pp. 1-21.

Vital, David (1969). "Back to Machiavelli." In Klaus Knorr and James N. Rosenau (eds.), *Contending Approaches to International Politics* (Princeton, NJ: Princeton University Press), pp. 144-157.

Wallace-Hadrill, J. M. (1985). *The Barbarian West 400-1000*, 4th ed. (Oxford, England: Basil Blackwell).

Wallerstein, Immanuel (1974) *The Modern World-System: Capitalist Agriculture and the Origins of the European World-Economy in the Sixteenth Century* (New York: Academic Press).

Wallerstein, Immanuel (1979). *The Capitalist World-Economy* (Cambridge, England: Cambridge University Press).

Wallerstein, Immanuel (1984). *The Politics of the World Economy: The States, the Movements, and Civilization* (Cambridge, England: Cambridge University Press).

Waltz, Kenneth N. (1967). *Foreign Policy and Domestic Politics* (Boston: Little, Brown).

Waltz, Kenneth N. (1979). *The Theory of International Politics* (Reading, MA: Addison-Wesley).

Waltz, Kenneth N. (1984). "Will the future be like the past?" In Nissan Oren (ed.), *When Patterns Change: Turning Points in International Politics* (New York: St. Martin's Press), pp. 16-36.

Wesson, Robert G. (1978). *State Systems: International Pluralism, Politics and Culture* (New York: Free Press).

Wiarda, Howard J. (1985). *Ethnocentrism in Foreign Policy: Can We Understand the Third World?* (Washington, DC: American Enterprise Institute for Public Policy Research).

Wilhelmy, Manfred (1984). "Politics, bureaucracy, and foreign policy in Chile." In Heraldo Muñoz and Joseph S. Tulchin (eds.), *Latin American Nations in World Politics* (Boulder, CO: Westview Press), pp. 45-62.

Williams, Penry (1981). *The Tudor Regime* (Oxford, England: Oxford University Press).

Worsley, Peter (1983). "One world or three? A critique of the world system theory of Immanuel Wallerstein." In David Held, et al., *States and Societies* (Oxford, England: Martin Robertson in association with The Open University), pp. 504-525.

Worsley, Peter (1984). *The Three Worlds: Culture and World Development* (Chicago: University of Chicago Press).

Young, Oran R. (1972). "The Actors in World Politics." In James N. Rosenau, Vincent Davis, and Maurice A. East (eds.), *The Analysis of International Politics* (New York: Free Press), pp. 125-144.

Young, Oran R. (1982). "Regime dynamics: The rise and fall of international regimes." *International Organization*, vol. 36, no. 2 (Spring), pp. 277-297.

Zinnes, Dina A. (1980). "Prerequisites for the study of system transformation." In Ole R. Holsti, Randolph W. Siverson, and Alexander L. George (eds.), *Change in the International System* (Boulder, CO: Westview Press), pp. 1-21.

Zolberg, Aristide R. (1981). "Origins of the modern world system: A missing link." *World Politics*, vol. 33, no. 2 (January), pp. 253-281.

Index

The idea of "the state" is so central to international relations, recognize the authors, that there is virtually no possibilty of developing unified and cumulative IR theory without it. Nevertheless, differing conceptualizations of the state cannot be bridged, because they reflect divergent political and ideological positions; from classical theorists to their present-day counterparts, efforts to define the state have inevitably combined views of what it is with what it ought to be. Ultimately, it is impossible to identify the essential qualities of the state by searching for it in history—not least because we cannot identify the phenomenon that is the object of the search.

Elaborating on this theme, Ferguson and Mansbach review the many meanings of the state. Since prehistoric times there has been a great variety of authority patterns evincing characteristics customarily associated with the modern state; institutional artifacts from every stage of human political evolution can still be found today; and many contemporary states are lacking the "state-like" qualities possessed by their European predecessors. A careful survey of current conceptions of the state reveals normative linkages, but also virtually no agreement as to the degree of state autonomy from internal and external constraints. The authors conclude that the concept of the state cannot contribute to—may indeed be detrimental to—the development to IR theory. Their proposed alternative is a "humanistic" agenda for theory-building that is firmly anchored in history, recognizes the existence of a wide range of political groups and loyalties, emphasizes behavior rather than institutions, and sees politics in a broad socio-economic and normative context.

Yale H. Ferguson is professor and chair of the Department of Political Science at Rutgers University, Newark. *Richard W. Mansbach* is professor and chair of the Department of Political Science at Iowa State University.